Ballast Books, LLC
www.ballastbooks.com

Copyright © 2023 by Michael Stutts

rights reserved. No part of this book may be reproduced in any form or by
electronic or mechanical means, including information storage and retrieval
ems, without permission in writing from the publisher, except by reviewers,
who may quote brief passages in a review.

ISBN: 978-1-955026-89-5

Printed in Hong Kong

Published by Ballast Books
www.ballastbooks.com

For more information, bulk orders, appearances, or speaking requests,
please email: info@ballastbooks.com

THERE'S NO ROOM SERVI

Psyc

Ward

From Boardroom to
Breakdown and Back

MICHAEL STUTTS

For all of my fellow insecure overachievers.

Insecure (insə'kyo͝or): Deficient in assurance; beset by fear and anxiety

Overachiever (ō-vər-ə-'chē-vər): One who achieves success over and above the standard or expected level, especially at an early age

Insecure Overachiever: "Exceptionally capable and fiercely ambitious, but driven by a profound belief in their own inadequacy" —Laura Empson

TABLE OF CONTENTS

CRY TOUGH

June 6, 2022

Watch this.

Kansas, Baylor, Virginia, Villanova, UNC, Villanova, Duke, UConn, Louisville, Kentucky, UConn, Duke, UNC, Kansas, Florida, Florida, UNC, UConn, Syracuse, Maryland, Duke, Michigan State, UConn, Kentucky, Arizona, Kentucky, UCLA, Arkansas, UNC, Duke, Duke, UNLV, Michigan, Kansas, Indiana, Louisville, Villanova, George-town, NC State, UNC, Indiana, Louisville, Michigan State, Kentucky, Marquette, Indiana, UCLA, NC State, UCLA, UCLA, UCLA, UCLA, UCLA, UCLA, UCLA, Texas Western, UCLA, UCLA.

That, of course, is the reverse order of all men's college basket-ball national champions from 2022 back to the UCLA run of the 1960s. You're just going to have to trust that I did that from memory.

I will pause while you gather yourself from the weight of what you just experienced.

This list has absolutely nothing to do with the topic at hand, though I would be happy to discuss it further. But it's a pretty good indicator of how my brain works:

1. I remember all kinds of stuff in great detail, even if sometimes I don't want to.

2. Rarely is it useful information.

3. I tend to meander and go deep into non sequiturs.

4. It never stops.

What should you take away from this?

1. If you ever need to know the questions on Terrible Testaverde's midterm that Screech knew from the lightning strike, then I'm your guy.

2. If you want to know today's date, I'm out.

3. Though my storytelling can be a bit winding, ultimately it gets where it needs to go.

Unfortunately, this constant brain churn and storage also makes the quiet time loud. I don't think my life has ever been quieter than it is right now. Ten weeks ago, I walked out of my fancy house and said goodbye to a hurricane of people, places, and bad habits that had formed and strengthened over fourteen years. Two weeks ago, I walked out of a psych ward and said goodbye to people and experiences that will live in my head and heart forever. Over the last few days, I've said hard good-byes to important people in my life who made a choice to abandon this ride, even after it pulled into the station. I don't fault them.

The best way I can explain being on the other side of intensive inpatient psychological treatment is that it's like waking up from a coma. Things look the same and feel like they should be the same, but almost everything in life is different. People moved through their own lives at regular speed while I lived what felt like three years during April and May of this year. I hit Ctrl+Alt+Del on myself, but because I was so full of viruses and trash, it was a slow reboot. My wheels spun for six weeks until I was ready to reenter the world and begin my processing duties.

For the last fifteen years, as a management consultant and C-suite executive, my life was nothing but noise. Airplane noise of two hundred flights per year. Voices of demanding clients, cranky senior partners, and unhappy junior staff. Even when I was asleep, I heard the sound of my brain grinding its gears, thinking of what I did wrong that day and what awaited me the next. When you're constantly trying to reach higher ground and achieve faster than your peers, life is loud.

Now, it's so quiet. The noises and people of a past life are gone. The minutes creep, and the hours crawl. I once wished weekends would stretch out forever. Last weekend finally did. I'm bored. I'm so, so bored. I know it won't last. My brain tells me as much. It whirs and buzzes and clicks and spins with rationality and wisdom that comforts and exasperates me, that makes me impatient. Add a healthy serving of Technicolor memories, many of which have been shaken to the surface like sediment in a lake, and you've got a large DQ Blizzard of emotion that you know you will eat all of, even if you don't want to. You just can't not.

In the last few weeks, these cookie dough chunks of feelings have yielded some long-abandoned behaviors. The main one is crying. Deep, heaving, can't-see-straight, Dawson-on-the-dock-after-Joey-chooses-Pacey type of crying. Big tears that are bad while driving. The most recent crying episode happened Saturday night after eating pizza and ice cream, watching *Candyman* (the OG one, not the 2021 remake), and playing late-night basketball alone. I did twelve-year-old Michael stuff as long as I could to distract myself from an empty hole in my chest, but I couldn't escape the inevitable waterworks on my couch at 11:45 p.m. Through blurry vision, I texted my sister/cousin/friend (we can't figure out which one it is), Emily, to find some safety in case things got worse. She was there—five hundred miles away, but there.

I spoke with my mom the next day. I was in the car, and she called me. The nice lady who meant well got a "let me be sad!" speech. I was indignant, passionate, and defiant in demanding I feel this emotion in all its magnitude. I didn't want to hear "It's for the best," and "You have so much to be thankful for." I wanted nothing more in that moment than to be sad. I asked her to imagine that my sadness was the flu and I was profusely vomiting into the toilet. Even though water would eventually be life-giving, it wasn't helpful to shove it down my throat while I was ears-deep in porcelain. The same was true for her well-intended words of comfort. I had to get the pain out before I could refill with spirit.

I just read all of that back. We've covered a lot of ground so far—sports, entertainment, bodily functions. But wow, it sounds pretty sad. And yet, I write this as a person who hasn't been this hopeful, optimistic, and free since I can remember. Buried in that dramatic emo account are coping mechanisms, self-care techniques, and emotional awareness that I learned while in the depths of my psychological despair. And importantly, I cried for the first time in years. I am finally feeling. No more self-medicating numbness or delusion that everything is fine. I'm finally me again. And I can still tell you the set list from the July 27, 2003, Bruce Springsteen show at Giants Stadium, so my brain is still there.

Writing all this down is a way for me to document the most turbulent and rewarding period of my life. I desperately sought achievement for decades, had a long-overdue breakdown, went to a psych ward, and came out better than ever on the other side. I know that I'm not the only one who has shut down their business career in the interest of mental health. I do think I'm one of the few sharing my story with the world. This book details the realities of walking into and living in a psych ward, relays the reasons I found myself there, and gives some practical guidance for how to balance career achievement and psychological serenity. It's pretty scary sending this lengthy message in a large bottle into the sea of the professional world while I'm in the middle of my career voyage. But if this document helps anyone, then it's worth the risk of my face landing on a corporate "do not serve" sign.

But let's be clear on this—I'm no clinician, psychologist, psychiatrist, or anything remotely resembling an actual authority figure in the realm of mental health. This is not a self-help book. And if you're using a book with numerous references to Guns N' Roses and *Saved by the Bell* as a medical guide, then perhaps you need a self-help book more than anyone.

So, welcome to the jungle of my memories, musings, and madness.

I.

Welcome to the Jungle

CHAPTER 1

SOMEBODY SAVE ME

There's a moment right when you wake up that brings a rush of information and context—a split second to take inventory of the where, when, what's real, and why you have to get out of bed. At 5:18 on a Thursday morning, I had one of those jolting awakenings and that wondrous mystery of "Where on Earth am I?" I generally love those because you start running through the good, weird, and worst-case scenarios. Then, finally, it all gels. This resolution fell into place with a loud voice and words that I knew individually but had never heard together, particularly directed at me: "Time to get your blood."

In that hazy instant, I saw a white ceiling, brown cabinets (with fake drawers that didn't actually function), and a bluish-gray carpet like the one in the "temporary" classroom trailers at Eastover Elementary. I felt two flat sheets fighting against each other. I heard a sound under my ear like crinkling paper in a plastic bag where a pillow allegedly was. I smelled nothing, absolutely nothing, the hallmark of a sterile hospital environment.

I woke up in a psych ward on the first of thirty-eight mornings to come.

With an emotional numbness and a sense of robotic duty, I exited the bed and slipped into my stylish, brand-new-but-modified Walmart shorts. No drawstrings allowed, and since I was born with a completely flat backside, I had to hold my shorts aloft as I donned my Carolina blue slip-ons (Vans, of course) for the short walk down the hall.

At home, I sometimes never saw a human for an entire day. On that morning, however, I was escorted by a nurse past a table of nurses into a room with a nurse. My sagging shorts and I slumped into a cold plastic chair. The hum in my ears was either the lights, a machine, or my groggy imagination. I was half asleep, and a cuff around my arm measured something or another. While I was staring blankly at the floor, a cold needle went into my right arm. I watched the blood flow into tube after tube. I knew what was happening, but I didn't particularly care why. I only hoped this was the worst of it, the lowest point of this experience. My liberty was gone. My compliance was expected. I would be jarred out of bed every day for a slow march to give blood (that last part turned out to be an exaggeration; it only happened one other time, but I was feeling dramatic).

The same nurse unceremoniously walked me back to my room. This time I was a bit more awake and felt every step of that journey. To my right, a brightly lit nurses' station had the clutter and activity of a busy medical unit. Above me, mirrors displayed hidden corners and crevices to unearth any potential surprises that a rogue resident may have in store. Blue and red lights adorned the ceiling outside of each room. I'm still not sure about their purpose, but they seemed medical and ominous. A black-and-white tag hung beside each door, bearing the half-remembered names of my new peers I had met the night before. The doors themselves were cracked open with washcloths jammed between the door and the frame. The centimeter of open space made it feel strangely communal and definitely not private. I would soon find out why I would do the same for my door.

I heard other shuffling feet, but I kept my head down. For some reason, it felt like I shouldn't look at the others. Maybe I just didn't want them to see me. It felt like when I was a kid shopping for underwear with my mom and saw a cute girl from school in the store—you're both there, you're both self-conscious and embarrassed, but hey, at least you're *both* mortified while you procure unmentionables.

I returned to my ultra-dull quarters at 5:31. I got the good news that I could go back to my slumber. Remounting the bed felt like putting on a button-down shirt with no sleeves. The sheets seemed designed to tangle and bunch on top of the mattress covered in plastic, for reasons I would rather not think about. I resumed my position of staring at the ceiling, checking all of my senses, and fighting off the racing, competing, and meandering thoughts that would inevitably take over.

I just woke up in a psych ward. I'm here. This is real. I'm not going anywhere anytime soon. What time do I have to wake up? What's that sound? What if I don't get better? I miss my home and my people. I'm going to wear this shame forever. "Leverage" isn't a verb; it's a noun. You don't "coverage" yourself with a blanket. Will I get along with anyone here? What am I missing at home? I'm exactly where I need to be. It was courageous of me to do this. Will people forget about me in here? There's no way that the Summer Roberts from the pilot episode would ever be with Seth Cohen; they had to change her character like 165 degrees.

I couldn't help but think of mornings in my past that were the direct opposite of what I was experiencing. I went back into the mind of the Michael who complained about ineffective blackout curtains in luxury hotels. Every hotel claims to have blackout curtains, but the true test is when you've been in seven time zones in less than a week. It's especially important if you've been in both the Northern and Southern Hemispheres and on three continents in the same time period. Your body feels like it's running the latest version of Windows on a 286 processor.

The Westin Paris Vendôme was always reliable in keeping the room dark. It's one thing I always appreciated about that hotel. The last time I was there, I felt thankful for the darkness, given that my previous hotel room in Santa Cruz do Sul—southern Brazil, tobacco country—had left much to be desired.

Brazil was a great trip, though. I joined a client to learn how their company operated in South America. This mainly consisted of visiting the families of local tobacco farmers to see their production process and way of life. Picture a small backyard crammed with tobacco plants, a shed where the leaves dry, and the whole family pitching in to move their household economy forward. We then toured the processing plant, which of course was a fascinating ballet of machinery that turned raw leaf into the stuff they put into cigarettes (and separated out the non-tobacco material, or NTM, which, on that day, included yellow nylon from a raincoat. I didn't want to know if someone was wearing the raincoat shortly before).

As with many facilities that I toured, the best parts of the process were at the beginning and the end. At the front end of this process, the local farmers brought their trucks full of raw leaf for weighing and grading by my client's staff of buyers. It was humbling to witness an entire family's year reduced to a single qualitative assessment and negotiation from a guy who looked at tobacco all day, every day.

Yet what happened at the end of the line was the real highlight. Quality control is a critical process in the tobacco production industry—just ask any North Carolinian. It's important to know that there are countless blends of tobacco that go into each finely tuned varietal of cigarette. Therefore, quality control must be nuanced and infallible. The process at this facility consisted of a blind man taking a pinch of each blend, hand rolling a cigarette, and smoking it to ensure a cool refreshing taste that made one Alive with Pleasure™.

The glamorous job that took me to this remote hub of tobacco production was that of a management consultant. Not just any management consultant but a partner and Managing Director, the highest order of the species. And I didn't work for just any management consultancy, but one of *the* management consultancies. My particular niche within the firm was that of "guy who isn't married and doesn't have kids so we can send him anywhere to do anything and it'll be okay." Within that niche, it was "guy who is redneck enough to work in industries like tobacco, fast food, and outdoor sports."

Becoming a partner was a multiyear process of mastering Power-Point, becoming an "expert" in twenty topics (the definition became looser by the day), and making myself at home in seat 3F. There is much to say about management consulting. I will say more as this book unfolds. One day, it will all be told in the definitive book about elite management consulting that someone will hopefully write. (Let's hope nobody writes that book. There is no place in the world for that book.)

Ten years of doing that job took me all over the world, which was great for a guy who hadn't left the country until age twenty-six. The Brazil trip was short, but not as short as my forty-eight-hour trip to Australia for a meeting that got canceled while I was on the flight. Definitely not as short as the time I flew to London for a day to sit in a room so that I could be "present" for an internal meeting that needed quorum. And not as long as the trips to Tokyo, Berlin, Dublin (Ireland), Dublin (Ohio), Dubai, Istanbul, and countless other magnificent destinations around the globe.

My favorite city was Paris. I always tried to make it there when I was in the neighborhood. The Westin was my home base. I loved to run from the hotel to the Eiffel Tower and back. It was exactly four miles. I felt at home there somehow. Sure, the Westin Paris isn't *the* nicest hotel in the area. But I was disappointed in the last Ritz I stayed in. And at least it wasn't as bad as when I had to stay at the InterContinental while my friends were at the Four Seasons in Prague. And don't get me started on the St. Regis in Rome, where room service ended at midnight when we absolutely *had* to have a gelato and fries at 2:00 a.m.

Waking up in the sterile, silent environment of the hospital was beyond humbling. It was scary. It was embarrassing. And it was terribly, terribly sad. In that moment, I couldn't help but compare the hospital-grade sheets to the Heavenly Bed dressings. I had to force myself to stop thinking about the day ahead of me and how it compared to past ones in Paris and Istanbul, full of fine steaks and wines. I wanted to cry, but I was too numb and emotionally exhausted. Just as I started feeling sorry for myself in my epic fall from five-star to functionally medical,

I remembered that one begat the other. I spent ten years in luxurious accommodations by night and in a psychological and physical nightmare by day.

I had no idea what awaited me on the other side of my slightly cracked-open door that day. I was comforted that while it may be unfamiliar, unsettling, and uncomfortable, it would be the first step toward recovery. For a moment, I was happy to trade the luxury for healing, even though I knew there wouldn't be chocolates on my pillow at the end of the night.

NOTHING'S GONNA
STOP US NOW

Please don't tell my sister Elizabeth that I intend to compare her to Tom Hanks. I don't mean it physically. I don't even mean it broadly. And even if I did, it wouldn't be the worst insult in the world. They are both very successful in their fields. They are talented and agile in their presentation. Elizabeth is just as comfortable at a music festival as she is at church; likewise, Tom can play an astronaut or a dimwitted shrimp boat captain. And it's not even the most ridiculous comparison between a family member and a Hollywood figure. One time a husky Midwestern man told my graceful, lovely, and definitively white mother that she reminded him of Morgan Freeman (he meant Morgan Fairchild).

Elizabeth and I rarely fly together, but we sure do love flying. We talk about planes often. We speak the language of flight as well as two dummies who have never seen a flight school can, and we even went to the Boeing factory in Everett, Washington, as birthday gifts to each other. Side note: we were born on August 14 and August 19 (not the same year, just to clarify). Our parents' birthdays are November 18 and November 22 (also different years but close). Feel free to do the grossest and most unlearnable math ever.

The only thing that excites and interests Elizabeth and me more than flying is plane crashes. Somehow around ten years ago, we figured out that we both love the show *Air Disasters* on the Smithsonian Channel. We discuss air crashes almost daily. It's extremely weird, particularly when you consider that the show airs on Sunday nights and I flew on five hundred Monday mornings during my consulting career. We aren't morbid people, nor do we celebrate carnage; we just want to know where the people who survived the crashes were sitting. We also really love stories in which one pilot domineers the other one. And we sure as heck are never, ever flying to Tenerife, Canary Islands (look it up—you'll know it when you see it).

On the morning of April 13, 2022, Elizabeth and I were flying Boeing 717 service on Delta to the city where I would be turned over to a mental hospital. Elizabeth had found a very highly acclaimed facility with a specific program that caters to professionals in times of crisis, which was precisely my context. The downside to this well-fitting shoe of recovery was that it was located several states west of my home in Tampa. No matter—I would have gone to Mars if it meant I'd get better.

We discussed our seating vis-à-vis what we knew about surviving a crash. We surveyed the plane for characters who would be featured on a show about a hypothetical crash. For a good episode, they'd need the lady across the aisle in the velour sweat suit holding a small dog, or the businessman talking loudly on his Bluetooth about closing deals. We evaluated whether one of the pilots seemed to be domineering the other. All systems go. To be clear, we really did not want to crash, unless it was a harmless one that would get us an interview alongside NTSB crash expert John Cox (our second-favorite TV guy besides Keith Morrison).

In that moment, I can't say I would have minded a minor air disaster that would have prevented me from reaching my destination. After several days of evaluating options, gaining admission (my insecurely overachieving self was nervous during evaluation calls for fear that I would be rejected from the psych ward, a feat that most would celebrate), and strategically packing a weird list of objects, I was on my way to getting better. The feeling was akin to standing at the start line of a half-marathon. You have prepared. You have committed to doing it, and you know you'll celebrate on the other side. There will be hills. There will be aid stations. There will be people with you on the journey. You'll have a cheering section. But you're the only one in pain, the only one who is accountable, and there are no shortcuts (I tried to find some when I ran those half-marathons, but no luck).

As I sat in the aisle seat (Elizabeth took the middle seat, but don't feel bad; she weighs 43 percent of what I do) and listened to soothing music with my eyes closed (*Kill for Love* by Chromatics; ten years later, it's still awesome), I couldn't help but think that we were in a scene from *Catch Me If You Can*, and I was the Leo DiCaprio (guy going to prison) to her Tom Hanks (FBI escort). I had felt like that for a week, since the day that Elizabeth flew to Tampa to take me to her home in Atlanta. Things had gotten extremely dire for me. We'll get to those details later; it's not pretty. What's critical to know is that:

1. I had communicated that I was ready to end my own life.
2. The only way I was able to eat, sleep, or think clearly was to drink a good amount of sauvignon blanc or rosé (I'm always in the Hamptons in my mind).
3. I had no family within a three-hundred-mile radius.

There wasn't enough Savvy B and Whispering Angel to sustain a lifetime of that behavior. Hence, Elizabeth to the rescue.

On the drive to Atlanta a few days earlier, we stopped at a Zaxby's for a healthy lunch of ~~salads~~ chicken fingers and fries. In what felt like my waning moments of freedom, I observed the post-church families, the hungover bros, and the diligent employees (one of whom left to go to her wedding after she took our order, no lie), and all I could think was that they were completely aware of my pathetic state and pitied me. They knew I was lost. They knew I was desperate. They could feel the shaking in my body, the need for help, the need for a visit with my friend Kim Crawford to straighten me out. They were so thankful that their lives were so simple, so stable, so problem free. And if something was wrong, at least it wasn't so bad that their big sister was transporting them across state lines.

At the airport and on the plane, this feeling magnified and multiplied. Now there were hundreds of best-life-living revelers going on awesome trips with family and friends without a care in the world. They all saw the handcuffs and chains on me and the *Pop-Up Video* bubble above my head with an arrow pointing to me, saying, "This dude is on his way to the nuthouse." The flight attendants were obviously concerned about my safety and that of the passengers. Their eyes showed the worry that I would break free and cause a scene, maybe try to pop that inflatable slide and tumble my way to freedom (bucket list item). Or perhaps I would rush to the cart, drink half of the airplane bottles, and shove the other half into various bodily hiding places to take with me. They skillfully restrained me in my seatbelt with consistent reminders that I needed to remain constrained by the seat-C shackles.

It wasn't important at the time that I was walking among glazed-faced, early-morning, business-traveling drones who had no knowledge or care of my condition or destination. All that mattered was my shame and distorted perception of reality, as well as doing whatever was humanly possible to delay walking into the facility. It wasn't that I didn't think I should go but that I was terrified of the uncertainty of the experience and my loss of freedom. On a normal day, I find it hard to walk into a fun party I'm invited to if I don't know who will be there and how easily escapable it will be. Thus, you can extrapolate my anxiety about having my legal guardianship turned over to people I'd never seen, in a place I'd never been.

Much to my dismay, there was no bird strike, engine failure, or catastrophic depressurization to stand in the way of an on-time landing. Thankfully, I had thought ahead regarding ways to disrupt a smooth operation. Once we landed, we had a thirty-minute drive to the facility, which of course could be reached via Uber, taxi, or even a reasonably healthy horse. In order to maintain my complete control and ability to delay my entry, I brilliantly rented a car in my name so that only I could drive it.

It turns out I am extremely skilled in stretching out a thirty-minute drive. Birds fly in straight lines. Normal people use GPS to find the most efficient route. I managed to come up with eight things that I "forgot" to pack that required eight stops at eight different retailers. Oops, no battery-powered alarm clock! How could I make it six weeks without every variety of Haribo gummy sustenance? We used 1.4 gallons of gas; we needed to replenish lest we become stranded. Elizabeth was obviously on to me at Target. I just *had* to use the bathroom and wash my hands profusely for at least ten minutes. Safety first. She told me she would wait outside the door of the bathroom and reminded me that there were no windows in the men's room.

After stopping at a Walgreens three U-turns away from the facility to buy a gigantic book of crossword puzzles, I could no longer stretch the commute. Elizabeth acted as the voice of reason and told me in a calm, objective, and reality-inducing way that it was time to go in. It was a very sad moment, but I knew she was right.

When we were kids, I would often verbosely ruminate about a decision and then seek Elizabeth's counsel about its resolution. Her additional three years of wisdom would be released in straightforward blurts. My five minutes of unloading would yield responses like "don't go," "break up with her," or "pop it." I never knew if her brevity was due to a lack of time, lack of patience, or just not wanting to deal with me for any longer than she had to. As an adult, I know it's that, in spite of experiencing so many of the same challenges as me, she is blessed with a clear and rational mind that makes people feel safe, cared for, and guided in the right direction.

She also knows how to drop a needle. As we approached the entrance, she didn't even have to ask what final song I wanted to hear before going in. "Everlong" by Foo Fighters, a song she and I had heard together live three times in the last twenty-two years, was perfect. It conjured thoughts of the recently departed Taylor Hawkins, a reminder that I still had life ahead and to make the most of it.

We had time for one more song. We listened to "Crazy Train" as we entered the gates. It only seemed appropriate.

CHAPTER 3

HYSTERIA

On March 30, 2022, I spent an entire day drinking sauvignon blanc. I was jobless with no responsibilities and intense feelings of uselessness and failure; a few gallons of Savvy B seemed like a good call. Never mind that weeks earlier, I had defiantly and shortsightedly fired myself while in a deteriorating psychological state—I still managed to conjure a sense of victimhood that called for a bender.

The bar was in a downtown restaurant set amid offices of bankers and lawyers. As neighboring finance bros and suited attorneys consumed their salads and Diet Cokes over lunch, I sat in a T-shirt and shorts, pounding white wine at noon on a workday. Surely these men wondered who this international man of leisure was, teeming with jealousy and awe of my carefree stance! If only they knew that it was a guy who, weeks earlier, was a sought-after, up-and-coming, in-demand C-suite executive who was skidding against his rock bottom.

That was a Wednesday. On Thursday I traveled to Chapel Hill, where I was attending a board meeting the next day. I was a bloated, hungover mess of a man, sweating in the only athleisure that fit me comfortably. I flew to Charlotte and finished the trip with a two-hour drive I had done many times in college. I hit the road around 7:15 p.m. I could barely function, possessed by a toxic mix of shame, regret, self-loathing, and hopelessness.

Throughout the first hour of the drive, my chest ached, my ears rang, and my vision was limited to what was three feet in front of me. Like a blind zombie, I inadvertently walked into the women's bathroom during a pit stop at the Pilot Travel Center. I could not formulate a coherent thought of my own. Instead, I only registered what I believed to be true: I was doomed to a life of misery, and there was no way out. I wasn't strong enough to break the cycle I was in. There were no sources of happiness available to me, even if I could muster the will to change. I had already brought enough irreparable shame to myself and my family over the last five years. Any more would break them. I had blown every romantic relationship, hurt partners and friends, and flamed out of two high-profile jobs. Everyone would have been better off without me in their lives. I was a net negative to the world.

I knew every exit, turn, speed trap, and high-quality gas station with clean bathrooms on Interstate 85 in the Piedmont of North Carolina. I also knew the most isolated parts of the route. I knew where there were bridges and obstacles close to the shoulder. An unbuckled seatbelt and a well-timed "accidental" loss of control of my rented convertible Mustang would turn the lights out, shut off my miserable thoughts, and leave no trace that the disaster was self-inflicted. There wouldn't be any guilt or "what ifs" in the hearts of those close to me. They'd play "Thunder Road" at my funeral (as is currently formally requested in a legal document). Some people would be sad, and everyone would move on. The only lasting casualty would be the decline of Whispering Angel rosé sales.

The fantasy was taking hold and becoming tantalizing. By the grace of God, I resisted going through with it. He gave me the image of my heartbroken mother and sister. He told me to be patient and that I was stronger than the evil urging of Satan, who wanted me to end my life and trick my family into thinking I didn't do it to myself. I limped into the AC Marriott Chapel Hill on Rosemary Street, jealous of the seemingly carefree and most likely non-suicidal patrons in the lobby bar. I could barely speak to the desk agent checking me in. He must have been confused and frustrated that I couldn't answer simple questions. I wondered what he would think if he knew my state of mind. Lately, I've been more empathetic to the behaviors of those who act strangely in public. You never know what they're going through.

I called my mother. I tearfully admitted everything that was happening. She convinced me to come to her house the next day instead of going home to Tampa. I managed to drive back to Charlotte and immediately collapsed on her bed. I wept in the fetal position for hours. I must have been the only former consulting firm partner and corporate executive mimicking the behavior of a three-year-old. I had completely given up. My mother took care of the pile of humanity I had become and soothed me into a Friday night's sleep.

The next day, I dutifully and foolishly powered through my agony and exhaustion to fly to New Orleans to attend the Final Four. I consider this to be a demonstration of the strength of The University of North Carolina Tar Heels' basketball rivalry with the Duke Blue Devils. They were facing off that night for the first time ever in the NCAA tournament, in the national semifinals no less. I rightfully believed it would be life-giving to be with old friends in an unforgettable setting and moment. For about twelve hours, these supporters kept me afloat without knowing it. Were it not for the shaking, sweating, and misery related to my brush with self-harm, it could have possibly been the best day of my life.

In deference to any Duke alums who may read this, I will not mention that UNC won the game in epic fashion, thus drawing the curtains on Coach Mike Krzyzewski's career. It would be beneath the level of expected decorum to remind the readers of the 81 – 77 final score. It should have been the single most triumphant moment of my sports fan life. Instead, I was scared silly when the buzzer sounded. The night was about to become unstructured on a Bourbon Street thick with alcohol, temptation, and the smell of urine. Pure physical exhaustion and an impending 7:00 a.m. flight mercifully sent me to my hotel room at a reasonable hour, unscathed and sober.

I called Elizabeth when I got home. She didn't flinch. We made a plan. She came to Tampa on Wednesday, April 6, to help me take back control of my life. I told her I needed to go away somewhere. I didn't know where but I had to do something serious. I had to disappear, to be contained, to be monitored. She agreed. She found a place and got the ball rolling. I was seven years old again, looking to my big sister in the hallways of Selwyn Elementary to give me confidence. She and I were back at our neighborhood creek, protecting each other from slippery rocks and emotional hurt from our changing lives. She was my protector, my friend, and the only one who could possibly know what I was going through.

On Sunday, April 10, we mothballed my Tampa life, packed my car, and drove to her home and family in Atlanta. So began the halftime of my life, and a chance to adjust my game plan for the second half to ensure a run to victory.

CHAPTER 4

LAND OF CONFUSION

Attending a live taping of *The Price Is Right* (which I've been fortunate enough to do twice, once with Bob and once with Drew) involves a very complex and opaque admissions sequence. It goes something like this:

- Get fired up for days. Make a homemade shirt, and study retail prices of mustard, party boats, and round-trip coach airfare from Los Angeles to Niagara Falls.
- Arrive at the CBS studio with little idea of what to do; look for other excited people in homemade T-shirts to give guidance on where to go.
- Follow signs into a corral where you're told, "They're always watching you."
- Line up by number. Get your ID checked, and fill out a form in case you win a fabulous prize.
- Queue into another line to get your yellow name tag made (fun fact: it has to be your legal first name, no exceptions).
- Relax for a bit. Be reminded that "they're always watching you," and learn that "they" are the producers who "watch you" through cameras to observe your behavior in line (be excited!!!!).

- Join another line, which surely is the one that leads to the studio and the models.

- Realize it's the line to be "interviewed" by the producers twelve at a time; do your best to sound super fired up and ready to play the dice game.

- Join yet another line, which must be the one that leads to the promised land of pricing games, but instead is another person telling you some rules and regulations.

- Browse the gift shop for CBS merchandise (no *Blue Bloods* Tom Selleck shirts, unfortunately) until you are finally escorted into the studio and shown a seat.

- Be overwhelmed, nervous, excited, and patient as you wait… wait…wait…wait.

- Finally stand up and cheer for the first four contestants coming down.

It turns out that the entry process into a mental hospital is similar, but not nearly as likely to result in winning a dinette set. After days of anticipation (but no homemade shirt), Elizabeth and I walked through the hotel-esque front doors to a receptionist, who incidentally must have a lot of fascinating stories. The room was inviting but not stimulating, welcoming but not cozy. The friendly staff member greeted us, slapped masks on us, and took my suitcase, backpack, and bags of procrastina-tion-driven retail items. Elizabeth agreed to not take any photos or tell anyone about the high-profile patients she saw. This all sounded very exciting. I started thinking about which celebrities going through a crisis I might befriend.

The staff member walked us through a door, which I was sure must have been the entry to the unit. I braced myself to see what my living space for the indeterminate future would be but instead entered a waiting room for incoming patients. The first of several waits began. All I can remember is brown. So much drab and nonthreatening brown. Brown wood, brown carpet, brown vision from my body in panic mode, reading an article about the Cleveland Browns considering a quarterback trade. A nurse approached me with a cart full of machinery. I would get to know this cart intimately in the weeks to come.

She took my blood pressure, oxygen levels, and temperature. It felt like *Dateline* when the people take lie detector tests. In thinking about not being nervous, I got even more nervous. The vital stats probably suggested I was near death. As an extra surprise, I received a blood alcohol content measurement. All of my intake conversations included my use of alcohol (which was not minimal, to say the least). It was wise of them to check this stat, but I was personally offended (or at least as personally offended as a person entering a psych ward can be). I was no alcoholic! I just needed booze to get me through several basic everyday functions for the last several weeks (as you can see, I liked to use my illusions liberally). I proudly wound up, blew into the tube, and clocked a 0.000 on the dial, which wasn't a surprise. It only made me wonder who held the record (the highest I heard from my cohort was 0.290 upon entry, which is terrifying and impressive).

With the diagnostics complete, surely it was time to go into the unit and see my new home and family? Not the case. Instead we were shown into an office where we met a quiet, calm, and inquisitive man who turned out to be the Chief Demoralization Officer. The next forty-five minutes consisted of him asking me every horrible personal question that I had already answered in my screening call. Am I suicidal at the moment? Am I drunk at the moment? Am I addicted to any prescription drugs? Do I have allergies, diseases, infections? Luckily, I learned to come up with good answers, as I was asked these same questions a few more times to come. They made sure I knew that my stay would be full of restrictions and lack of control (my two biggest fears). He was a kind man who meant well. I knew that. But you know those teachers who smile, put a cat sticker on your test, and give you a D-minus? That was this guy.

This interaction brought the first scary moment, one that made me so grateful Elizabeth was with me. In keeping with my apparent new branding as an alcoholic, this fella informed me that I would have to take a medication that brought patients down from their intoxication and limited their withdrawal symptoms. That I blew a goose egg on the breathalyzer and showed no other signs of withdrawal were irrelevant. I was in no shape to fight (typically, tears coming out of one's eyes diminishes one's negotiating power), so Elizabeth puffed up on my behalf.

One of the biggest fears that she and I both had about this experience was overmedication and zombification. We were not here for it. Elizabeth was logical, tough, and persistent. I was confused, frightened, and fragile. In the end, I called off Elizabeth's efforts and submitted to the process. I didn't have any more emotional energy to give, and I had to assume this man would not steer me toward some sort of experimental medication. In the end, we respected his credentials and professional opinion (plus, the meds ended up giving me a sweet little buzz to get me through the first twenty-four hours).

I signed roughly 2.3 billion sheets of paper that made me a possession of the hospital and made them responsible for my well-being. I had new guardians, at least for a little while. This was a bizarre reality. It was a feeling that I was too numb to process at the moment.

Finally, our time with Danny Downer was over. Surely it would be time to ooze into the unit and plop on a chair? But no, we went to yet another waiting area and another brown office on the "unlocked" side of the building. This time, it was with a lovely woman who walked us through some of the logistics of living there, how I could communicate with home, and of course the billing process. It turned out they did not accept Marriott Bonvoy loyalty points as payment.

This lady was wonderful. She was comforting and sensitive, and she gave us space to feel our emotions. I can't speak for Elizabeth, but I can't imagine it was easy dropping her little brother off at an overnight psychiatric camp. It didn't help that I was like an emotional washing machine cycling through noisy modes. There was the CCCCCSSSHH-HHHHH mode in which I asked pointed questions and challenged rules I was told. Then the WHHUMMMMMMMMMM mode, consisting of Elizabeth and me laughing at anything in which we could find humor.

Next came the ERRRRR-PPPHMM stage when my body became numb, my breathing became broken, and tears ran down my face.

Our time in that office would be our last together. Elizabeth prayed over me. I wept. Elizabeth was strong. We walked out of the office back to the lobby. We hugged. She gave me words of encouragement. She led by example with smiles and unwavering words. She walked out the front door. It was the last time I'd see a familiar face for a long time. I had dreaded that moment, but it was over, and I survived.

This time, I was certain the next door we walked through would lead into my highly anticipated hospital unit. But no, this one was like the Willy Wonka door that leads to the chocolate waterfall room. At least, insomuch as I didn't expect to walk through a locked, alarmed, metal door into a very large, beautiful, and serene courtyard. The grounds were bright green and well manicured, complete with mature trees and blooming flowers. I couldn't see where it ended. It was so quiet—no car sounds, no yelling, only birds chirping and wind rustling through branches. There were grassy knolls, park benches, shady spots under trees, and a circular maze for meditative walking. I found out that I would not be able to use any of these features for weeks, as freedom of movement in nature was earned through consistent rule compliance, recovery progress, and twenty-one sunrises and sunsets. That said, it felt like a place I could really enjoy for a while.

The courtyard was circular, with sidewalks crisscrossing and surrounding it, but I didn't see any people walking. It was only me with my assigned nurse escort, who was rolling one of those hotel luggage rack things. I had no idea where we were going. I felt like one of the new fish walking into Shawshank. I really hoped Bogs wouldn't be waiting for me. I am pretty good with numbers, so maybe the warden would give me an opportunity to launder and embezzle. And perhaps there would be a Red to befriend me and acquire things on my behalf. It was the most nerve-racking and painfully slow walk of my life.

At long last, after a seemingly endless march of about fifty yards, we reached the glass door of my unit. I passed through the locked outer door and walked down a long, bland hall with three locked doors on the right. No smells, no sounds, no cat posters. The end of the hall had another locked glass door, but just before it there was a window into the nurses' station, kind of like when you're leaving the doctor and you pay and set your next appointment that you'll definitely cancel. I stopped there and handed off all of my belongings from the luggage cart. I also handed over my iPhone, but not before several furious last-second texts to my mom, my sister, and my yard guy. It was like yelling out of a train window as it leaves the station. That was a traumatic experience. I may as well have surrendered my hands themselves.

At long last, the final door opened, and I walked into the unit, my new home for the next six weeks. The unit was T-shaped, with the door at the top left of the crossbar. The intersection of the crossbar and the pole of the T housed a large nurses' station that extended back into a restricted zone. If you looked straight at it without looking to the left or right or behind you, it felt exactly like a hospital. Which, of course, it was.

The crossbar of the T was a long, carpeted hallway with bedrooms on either side. In theory, women were on one side of the nurses' station and men on the other, but we were pretty dude-heavy during my time on the unit. Picture a college dorm hallway with white walls and brown doors, and you've pretty much got it. There were twenty total bedrooms lining the halls. One side of the hall had views of the aforementioned courtyard, while the other side featured vistas of a large fence that separated the campus from an apartment complex. I had two rooms during my stay, one on each side. There were far fewer dog barks and fireworks on the courtyard side.

The vertical section of the T was a large, open, and very high-ceilinged common room. We're talking three-story-high ceilings, the kind that makes you feel small and sounds seem big. For reference, the best thing to picture is a public library in 1997. Lots of natural light supplemented by fluorescent light, white walls, brown furnishings, and a low murmur of noise. There was a ping-pong table, a brownish red couch (identical to couches I've seen in fraternity houses that effectively hide stains—gross), and a handful of study lounge-ish chairs pointed toward a reasonably large television. If you kept your back to the nurses' station, you could see a bookshelf on the immediate right and three clunky desktop computers on the immediate left. Further toward the back, there were windowed rooms off of both the left and right side. These would become a big part of my life. The back wall was full of windows that framed a small courtyard and garden specific to our unit, complete with lounge chairs and tables (all of which were surrounded by a twelve-foot brick wall with laser sensors on the top).

An important feature of the entire complex was that it was all on a single level, which meant that for six weeks I didn't use stairs, escalators, elevators, dumbwaiters, or the motorized chairs that old people use. This fact did not hit me until months later, as I was walking down a steep metal staircase at a music festival. There are little moments and reminders of life in the clinic when you're out in the real world that can hit you hard.

I entered the unit sometime between 2:00 p.m. and 2:30 p.m. on a Wednesday. I know this because at that time every week, there was a community meeting attended by all of the patients and staff. It was usually about twenty-five to thirty people gathered in the common room, basically a town hall, to talk about the goings-on and requests of the unit. I managed to walk in during the single thirty-minute window of each week when every last eyeball was gathered in one spot to check out the new guy.

This took me back to second grade, when my mom walked me into the classroom of my new school. All of the fundamental insecurities come rushing back, except this time my peers didn't have to imagine something was wrong with me—they knew that something definitely was. I felt their eyes on me, and I knew they were wondering whether I was an addict, suicidal, a melter downer, an angry dude, or maybe something cool they'd never heard of (I can confirm that these are the unstated mental questions when a new person walks in).

Instead of meeting any of these folks, I was swept into a series of meetings with doctors and nurses. Step one was a physical. Standard vitals, EKG, body check, partial nudity, crippling insecurity, unsolicited overexplaining my lack of perfect fitness, the usual. Next, a lovely chat with a psychiatrist to review yet again all the reasons why I was there, which medications I was taking, and whether I was going to be super excited and unstable or mimicking a puddle for the first twenty-four hours. I regretted to inform him that I would not make an awesomely wheels-off scene and would instead resemble Jell-O. Finally, I endured a quick meeting with a few of the nurses to once again review all my defects and recount a rousing tale of my recent unraveling.

The rapid-fire battery of evaluation ended with a release into the wild of the common room. I was given no further instruction and had absolutely no idea what to do. The feeling was certainly familiar. I've walked into a lot of cocktail parties and networking events in my day, many of which were devoid of any familiar faces. I generally hate them all from start to finish, but by far the worst part is the super awkward wandering around to find the least stuffy group to break into. I did my best milling about, half-smiling, head-nodding, and fiddling with papers and notes to look like I had purpose.

I was saved by the first of my new friends—a kind man named Floyd who literally extended a hand of friendship. He was wearing a black shirt with the *Dark Side of the Moon* prism thing and the lyric "I have become comfortably numb." In my best attempt to connect, I said, "Oh hey, you're a rock 'n' roll guy," to which he plainly informed me that it was his special shirt he wore on his ketamine treatment days. A valiant connection effort was thwarted, but Floyd and I got along famously over the next several weeks. To this day, he is one of the kindest and most selfless people I've ever met.

I continued my drift about the unit and stopped at the bookshelf, which was somewhat of an indicator of what I was walking into. It was full of the most haphazard collection of literature, most of which was left behind by previous residents over the years. The content and arrange-ment of the books was telling of the people and place. There were page-turner mass-market fiction books, several bibles and Christian books, a slew of books on art and games, a lot of psychology and addiction-help books, and the autobiography of the MyPillow guy. It was clear that, at some point, there had been an attempt to alphabetize the books. Knowing what I know now, it was likely a weekend project by an industrious individual to pass the time with a mindfulness activity. Or it was quite possibly the work of a patient with hardcore OCD.

My aimlessness came to an end when two nurses showed me to my new quarters. Think of a cruise ship cabin, but replace cheerful Caribbean regalia with various shades of brown. Then remove all electronics, and modify everything in the room such that there is no possibility that the occupant could hang themselves. No drawers, no clothes hangers or rods, no doorknobs, no fitted sheet, and no corded devices. The bathroom was equally safe and weird. No shower curtain rod, no faucet, no glass, and no showerhead (it was a fixed nozzle that supplied a direct stream of water to the shoulder of my six-foot-four frame).

Great care went into making our environment a secure one, which meant that it had absolutely nothing that could be dangerous even to the most creative mind. The nurses sat me in a chair squeezed between the bed and the window to endure a humiliating search of my belongings. I had received a very comprehensive list of items to bring and not bring, kind of like summer camp but without the bug spray (which was expressly prohibited). Here are the basics:

- No drawstrings (every time you cut the drawstrings from a pair of lululemon shorts, a yoga instructor sheds a tear).

- No shoelaces (this place was a dad shoe fashion show—Crocs, Vans, and various hideous choices).

- No belts (I assumed that formal dinner night with the captain would be canceled).

- No offensive T-shirts (how would everyone know how cool I was without my Big Johnson shirts?).

- No revealing clothing (so much for my mesh, cutoff tank tops).

- No clothing with alcohol, tobacco, or drug references (my Marlboro jacket had drawstrings anyway).

- No toiletries with dangerous ingredients (I've always wanted an excuse to use No More Tears shampoo again).
- No toiletries in glass containers (six weeks without Drakkar Noir or nail polish would be brutal).
- Obviously, no knives, guns, or weapons of any sort (including the indefensible nail clippers).
- No laptops, phones, or DVD players (or presumably pagers, Walkmen, Sidekicks, and fax machines).
- No corded headphones or cords of any kind (so much for my rotary phone idea).

I'd dutifully adhered to this list, or at least I thought I had. I left anything that I thought would be forbidden in my backpack, which I incorrectly assumed would be thrown unchecked into a secure closet and not be seen until departure. Instead, the nurses went item by item through said bag that, for ten years, I had carried across five continents.

A detailed inventory of the excavation:

- Several pens in various states of decay.
- Fifteen USB thumb drives, many of which featured defunct company logos.
- Seventy-three cents.
- Keys to unknown locks.
- Wrinkled printouts of a PowerPoint from a meeting in 2017.
- A single gummy bear.
- The last of my dignity.

With my contraband fully accounted for and safely stowed, all that was left was for me to put away my meager belongings in the room and do my best to make myself at home. When I was on the road in the consulting job, I made a habit of spreading my stuff around to the maximum extent to make any hotel room look well inhabited and homely. That was harder to do in this case. I only had about fifteen pieces of clothing (a sock-inclusive number), and room cleanliness was strictly enforced. I stashed my garments onto the shelves and displayed a few pictures and keepsakes that reminded me that I was me. Then, for the first time during this whirlwind, I was alone, stationary, and in silence. It became real. This was my home.

My little pity party was mercifully interrupted by a daily check-in meeting with the patients at 5:00 p.m. I was finally able to meet my cohort, of which I was the eighth member (that number had grown from four a few weeks earlier and would eventually rise to thirteen during my stay and drop to nine by the time I exited). At first glance, the group was younger than I expected (mostly aged forty to fifty), seemed more "normal" than I expected, and was dressed in a wide array of creative and code-compliant athleisure.

Every morning and evening during these meetings, each member of the group said their first name, where they were from, what they were looking forward to (morning meeting), and what their best part of the day was (evening meeting) and answered a silly/inquisitive/random check-in question. It was a nice ritual that marked another day underway or complete, one that brought forced-and-appreciated companionship to what could be a lonely place.

"My name is Michael. I'm from North Carolina. The best part of my day was that I actually made it in here. I'd rather it be cold forever because you can add clothes if you're cold, but there are only so many you can take away if you're hot."

My peers hailed from all US time zones and had a host of purposes for being there. At the time, there were five men and three women ranging from their late twenties to their late sixties. Most were in the prime of their careers, but some were recently retired, and one was a student in a high-pressure graduate discipline. The group included people who were married, single, divorced, about to be divorced, or would be divorced if this stay didn't go well. In the first thirty minutes of knowing them, I heard laughs, tasted my own tears, felt handshakes and hugs, saw smiles and kindness, and became comforted that everything would be okay (if a little weird at times). Everyone brought their own baggage. Nobody had room or desire to judge, and each person would handle their journey in the way that made sense for them. I had to figure out mine.

I kept hearing about giving in to the environment, the process, and the progress. I didn't know what that meant. I didn't even know how to make a bed without a fitted sheet. But I was here. I was part of this group, albeit eating dinner alone that night because I wasn't allowed to leave the unit for the first twenty-four hours. I don't remember what was on the tray. I didn't eat it. I hadn't eaten in a full day. I picked at the food politely even though nobody was looking or cared. That's just the kind of guest I am.

The rest of the night, a firehose of information and guidance was given from the other patients in exchange for clues I might reveal as to what kind of neighbor I would be. I didn't know exactly how I'd contribute to and live within the group as yet, so they would have to wait. I received invaluable information about the various tips, tricks, and hacks of the unit. A man named Pablo was assigned to be my "mentor" for my first few days, as was his charged task in the group (everyone had a role or two, including yours truly, who ascended to the office of the presidency. More on that later). Pablo was immediately a kind and welcoming new friend who quickly became a close confidant. I just texted him a few minutes ago.

He told me of countless rules and regulations, what we could and couldn't do, daily processes and rituals, some of the unspoken etiquette, etc. But by far the most important things I learned and put into practice that night involved sleep. I was told to immediately order new pillows and a mattress topper, but in the meantime to take the existing awful pillow, wrap a towel around it, put the cases from both pillows on the one pillow in opposite directions, and then forget the other pillow existed. This would alleviate the newspaper-in-a-trash-bag feel of the standard-issue headrest. Next, he instructed me to take a washcloth from the bathroom and stuff it between the door and the frame. This would make the middle-of-the-night check-ins less noisy.

Middle-of-the-night check-ins, you say? The letter of the law of that state is such that in a psychiatric facility, every patient must be accounted for with proof of life every *fifteen minutes*. This is a 24/7 rule, including sleep, shower, and toilet. I can't believe that I can say I got used to the door cracking open and a bath of red light (expert tip: sleep with your back to the door) four times an hour. In fact, it was hard to get used to not having it when I got home. But I have never missed yelling "I'm alive!" while taking care of business in the bathroom.

I made it through my first day via a combination of will, knowledge that I had no other option than to be there, and whatever that pill had been that made me feel two White Claws deep. All that was left was to creep into a room full of my peers and watch the movie *Trainwreck*, which seemed somehow appropriate (but not quite as on-the-nose as *One Flew Over the Cuckoo's Nest*, which we *actually watched* weeks later just to be as cliché as possible).

Halfway through the movie, I was done. I promised everyone I would be better in the future and stay up with them. I had no idea if this was true. I just didn't want to disappoint them. I wanted them to like me. I had to make them like me. If they didn't like me, then how could I be fulfilled? How could I be a valuable member of society if they weren't laughing at my jokes, respecting me, and wanting to be my friend?

Imagine a world where it is possible to be a happy person without needing validation from everyone around you, even those far away. Imagine not having to constantly prove your worth and success in the eyes of people who are dead. Imagine not needing to constantly refuel, regardless of how it makes others feel. And imagine not needing any chemical assistance to provide the energy, boldness, and numbness required to fuel these needs and numb the pain that you cause.

Now, imagine a bedroom so bereft of electronics and stimulus that all you had was a spinning mind full of your own uncertainties, insecurities, and all-out fears. Imagine having no way to communicate with the people you've relied on, unfairly or not, to get you through your pain even if you're not acknowledging theirs. Imagine being too afraid to tell the truth about your habits and behaviors to these people but knowing you will have to face that reckoning once you get out of this place. Imagine knowing you'll lose them.

Imagine a terrible, crinkly pillow loud enough to drown out most of these thoughts, but not all of them.

Now you can picture what it's like to go to bed as a broken toy in a mental institution.

CHAPTER 5

I THINK WE'RE ALONE NOW

When I was in high school, we had the most complicated schedule ever. It was a seven-day schedule with six periods of varying length, day to day. We got out early on Tuesdays for some reason. To make it a bit easier, we went to the same class first period every morning, except for the mornings that we didn't. To this day, I have a recurring dream about not knowing which class I have next, unable to find my schedule. Frequently, I'm not wearing pants and carrying my childhood stuffed animals. That's a whole other neighborhood of psychoanalysis.

At the clinic, we had a similarly rigidly structured daily schedule, albeit much, much simpler. The prevailing theme was order. Every morning was the exact same—wake up at 7:45 a.m., journal, read a daily devotional, walk to the nurses' station to take vitals (blood pressure + temperature + blood oxygen), get medications from the window (yep, it's just like the movies, except they don't check under your tongue like they did for Sarah Connor in *Terminator 2*), grab a granola bar and OJ, start the morning check-in with the peer group at 8:30 a.m. Every meal was at the same time every day. Evening peer check-in was every night at 5:00 p.m. It was clockwork. I had never experienced anything like it.

The best way to think of the entire program is to imagine being a first year in college—everyone has a core required curriculum. The rest of the schedule is based on your "major" or area of interest, whether it's addiction, post-traumatic stress, eating disorders, or something else. Everyone lives and eats together. However, there are also many, many, many ways in which an inpatient program at a mental hospital differs from college.

The foundation of the daily and weekly schedule was psychotherapy. That should be obvious. Every week included a battery of one-on-one sessions: one with our psychiatrist (the one who can prescribe meds), three with our psychologist (the one who listens, talks, analyzes, and stares at you silently as if he is burning a hole through you like the villains in *Superman II*), and one with our social worker (the one who gets to the bottom of your family and relationship drama). We also had group therapy sessions twice a week, plus additional classes with our peers that were more about education and less about processing. Together, we learned tools and techniques for handling our issues at a high level. The two best examples from my early days are learning to talk to myself as if I were talking to a friend in need and counting items in the room to bring my mind to the present instead of swirling about in the past or future.

As for the "electives," each patient attended one-on-one sessions and groups focused on individual areas of need. We had a couple of suicidal people, a handful of substance abuse folks, those who suffered from eating disorders, and a lot of trauma survivors. These sessions were intense in every way, including how quickly you got to know some of the darkest components of your peers' lives. It's rather surreal to learn everything a person doesn't want the world to know in a matter of seventy-two hours.

Beyond the hard work, we had scheduled meals, exercise, community meetings, creative outlets (I went to arts and crafts exactly once, where I painted a birdhouse; it was the only time I truly felt like a crazy person) and scheduled leisure time to do whatever we chose to do. Some people napped, while some checked emails on our fancy desktop computers, and some obsessed over crossword puzzles (I got good).

In the first week, time is very slow. Everything feels unfamiliar and sometimes a bit scary. We were constantly asked to talk about ourselves, our histories, our pains, and a lot of things we tried to forget over the years. I thought of things I didn't know that I remembered. All of this brain activity was exhausting, not only in the moment but also residually in sleep. My dreams became more vivid and bizarre by the night. It was like my brain was a snow globe that had sat on a shelf for decades, and someone was now shaking it, stirring the shimmering plastic flakes from the bottom to the top of the sphere.

By the end of the first week, the narrative of how I ended up locked in a clinic started to take shape. It took the full six weeks and more to work out the details. So begins the melodrama.

II.

Raised
on Radio

CHAPTER 6

nO ONE IS TO BLAME

For people my age, one of the lasting cultural mainstays of our college experience was MTV's TRL. Fun fact: the original TRL that aired in the late '80s was called Dial MTV. The premise was that people at home would call a 1-800 number (you'll never guess what it was) and request their favorite videos, which I suppose was the exact premise of what occurred in the Spears/Aguilera/LFO era. I know this because every night Elizabeth and I would tune in to see the finest and most-requested songs that pop culture had to offer. Esoteric think pieces like "I Want Your Sex" by George Michael accompanied late-peak Journey arias like "Girl Can't Help It" to create a soundtrack for our rec room. "Rec" was, of course, short for "recreation," and "room" was a loose term to describe a former garage that had been carpeted and insulated with minimal effort. The primary recreation consisted of the two of us ingesting glorious MTV trash and eating junk food with health content and taste commensurate to the bloated hair metal and sugary pop music. We loved it.

The freedom to consume 1987 entertainment with limited oversight accelerated the formation of my cultural taste. For the whole of my first six years, I was exposed only to smooth adult contemporary rock and R & B about love, forbidden beaches, and forlorn middle-aged men. Thirty years later, it would come to be known as yacht rock. Think

Michael McDonald, Hall and Oates, pre-"Danger Zone" Kenny Loggins, and you get the idea. My earliest favorite songs were "Rosanna" by Toto, "If Ever You're in My Arms Again" by Peabo Bryson, and "Say You, Say Me" by Lionel Richie. Don't get me wrong; all of these songs were bangers then and still are today, but they weren't exactly what the kids were listening to. As far as I knew, what played on EZ 104.7 in my mom's Buick Electra station wagon (with a forest's worth of wood paneling) was the entire musical universe.

With MTV opening my seven-year-old eyes and ears, my musical palette developed into two primary nodes: hair bands (Poison, Mötley Crüe, Van Halen, et al.) and middle-aged men who were still allowed to be pop stars in the late '80s (Steve Winwood, Phil Collins, Billy Joel, and other decidedly unsexy forty-plus-year-olds). There was something exciting about having a leather-and-motorcycles side and a clean-cut, safe-for-daughters side. I wanted long hair and a flying V guitar while also playing golf with Huey Lewis and the News. While I was unabashed about my lean toward metal sleaze, there was one band that prompted a quick channel change if Mom came into the room. Guns N' Roses was a freight train of beautiful, terrifying noise and dangling-from-lips cigarettes. It blew me away. It scared me and thrilled me. And man, did I want to know more about the Jungle and why adults hated these guys so much.

I was also a growing boy with hormones emerging from their latent cocoon. I never admitted it, but I was always excited when the fans dialed MTV for Belinda Carlisle, my ultimate crush with the ultimate key-changing anthem, "Heaven Is a Place on Earth." That jam soundtracked many a daydream about young love, which I imagined was holding hands with a girl and sitting in the cafeteria together (neither of which I actually accomplished). Love was confusing when you were taking in Madonna's one-two pelting of age-inappropriate content in "Papa Don't Preach" and "Open Your Heart." I learned more than I needed to know about reproductive decisions (though for a while I thought she wanted her father to quit his church job) and the risk of being an adolescent boy who sneaks into a peep show (watch the video—it's *To Catch a Predator* level of creep).

My musical discovery translated beyond the rec room and into home décor and second-grade leisure activities. Amid bedroom posters of Countaches and Testarossas were large-scale photos of Jon, Richie, Tico, Bryan, and Alec to remind me of how freaking much I loved Bon Jovi. Jon himself graced an enormous poster on the exterior-facing part of my bedroom door, or at least it did for a few days before it was deemed one click too ridiculous (one of the few limits enforced on me). Imagine the immeasurable elation emitting from my pasty little body when, on March 25, 1987, I was allowed to attend the Bon Jovi concert at the Charlotte Coliseum. We rocked from Cinderella's opening set (capped off by "Nobody's Fool") until late into Bon Jovi's set, when we made our sleepy-kid exit. I did my best to mimic the rock 'n' roll fan moves I had seen in the "Livin' on a Prayer" video. Double fist pumps, "yeeeahhh!!" screams, and "we'll give it a shot!" sing-alongs. I'm sure Elizabeth and our big sister-esque babysitter Maebeth were horrified. Bet your Lunchables that I wore a concert tee to school the next day (yep, it was a school night—a Wednesday, to be exact).

It wasn't just music that we took in. We also loved (and were questionably allowed to watch) MTV culture-adjacent movies. Well, we mostly watched what Elizabeth chose. A whole lot of *Dirty Dancing*, *The Lost Boys*, and *License to Drive* made me excited and terrified to be a teenager. Was I supposed to think that being a vampire was cool? Did teenage girls really like middle-aged dance instructors? *Mannequin* was among the most confusing movies, as it seemed to give permission to create your own reality and your own girlfriend. My strengthening draw to music put me squarely in the sights of *La Bamba*. Never before nor since has there been a better performance from Esai Morales. Looking back on it, it's pretty hard to believe that kids my age were rocking out to Los Lobos singing cover versions of 1950s songs.

We only consumed these movies and music videos after all outdoor activities were no longer possible. The daily ritual was always the same. We walked the mile or so from Selwyn Elementary to our flagrantly 1960s-style ranch home, dropped off our bags, waved hello to Mom, and then determined the afternoon agenda. There were a few options:

maybe play basketball, perhaps scale the easily climbable greenhouse to hang out on the roof, perhaps ride bikes to the Hemingways' house to see what they were up to.

Elizabeth and me emulating our MTV influences
(hard to say which artist in this case)

The creek walk was the GOAT of our elementary school afternoon agenda. Our home sat next to a small waterway that, to us, may as well have been the Mississippi River. Our neighborhood friends would meet at the launch point in our yard. Then we'd hop the rocks, tree roots, and sewer pipes to traverse up the various stages of the mighty, trickling artery. The first leg of the walk was easy, and after a while we knew how to get past the tiny "rapids" to the big pool at the bend where the banks grew further apart. Here, you could actually feel the water rushing in the ten-yard-wide creek. This was where things got treacherous. There were large slippery rocks that could bridge us to the firmer land on the opposite side, but we might also slip and go waist deep in cold and dirty water. We might earn a talking-to from Mom or a tough case of flesh-eating bacteria, not to mention bruised egos and rear ends. By the time we got to the office building near the mall, we'd gone as far as we could and have to turn around. The walk back always seemed shorter than the hike out. I guess that's always the case with any adventure.

Summers altered our routine, but it was still the two of us in charge of our domain. Along the creek ran a worn footpath that connected our quiet street with a more trafficked road that led to our local pool. We walked that trail daily all summer, joined by some neighborhood friends and not-so-friends (the ones who stole stuff from our backyard) to the Barclay Downs Swim and Racquet Club. This was your typical gathering place for restless kids, stay-at-home moms, and lazy baby-sitters who wanted to kill time. From late morning until daily sunburn, we would wrinkle ourselves while horsing around in the T-shaped pool, show off on one of the last high diving boards in existence, and cap it off with two dollars' worth of the finest Lance-branded products from the snack bar. This was the beginning and end of the summertime social scene. I revered the older kids, these thirteen-year-old kings and queens who set the tone and the unwritten rules. No clearer was this leadership than in the jurisdiction of the four-square court. You couldn't come weak to that scene, and you'd best know all of the stupid and arbitrary regulations set in real time by the older kid who'd sooner burn their Umbros than relinquish their King square. These days at the pool flew by, but we knew we'd see our friends and crushes soon enough the next day.

Whether we were leaving the creek or the pool, we'd walk back to home base when the streetlights began to glow. We'd triumphantly reenter our kingdom, establish ourselves in the rec room, and dine on either frozen pizza or whatever my mom made that day at work. Our mom had a pretty cool job. She was a television pioneer in Charlotte and part of a broader movement in America. After being a flight attendant and a schoolteacher, she tried out for a role on TV, and against all odds (you're thinking about Phil Collins, aren't you?), she got the role. Not only that, but she became the highest-rated female personality in Charlotte and an up-and-coming commodity nationally.

Her primary gig was co-hosting the midday news and variety show called *Top O' the Day*, on which she interviewed national celebrities and local people of interest. Her real strong suit and claim to fame was the daily cooking segment. At the time, she had just published her second cookbook and was the 1987 version of a cooking influencer. Going to the grocery store with her was like walking Abbey Road with Paul McCartney. Every school night, she cooked a dish featured on the next day's show, and each following night, we had the option of dining on whatever concoction she featured. Of course, not all the dishes were hits. The unappetizing irony was that the only food that came home was the weird cuisine that was spurned by the hungry camera crew, so often Elizabeth and I utilized our veto power.

The amount of influence and autonomy Elizabeth and I had gave us confidence and made us leaders among our peers. We were the new kids in the neighborhood and at Selwyn Elementary. While Elizabeth didn't need a second-grade brother in a classroom down the hall, it built my confidence to have a cool sister in the fifth grade. We were quick to make friends and adapt to our new environment, skills that would come in handy later in life. We were cheerful, adventurous, and creative kids with a mom on TV and stylish Benetton clothing our backs. We looked like the postcard version of late-Reagan-era kid paradise.

Under the façade, however, we were two kids navigating seismic changes in every facet of our existence. A year earlier, our lives were entirely different. We lived in a tree-lined neighborhood in the house that had welcomed us home from the hospital, the house that our beloved Archie (my mom's dad) had built, the last and only house where we had both parents present. It was the only world we knew for our first years, and we liked that world just fine.

I'm gifted and cursed with a brain that retains unnaturally crisp and bright memories of my first six years, the ones where my mom, my dad, Elizabeth, and I lived under the same roof. I remember sleeping in my crib, particularly waking up criminally early and hollering for my mom while holding the bars. My dad would come in and tell me that Mommy was still at work but she would be home soon. At the time, my mom was doing the early morning show on the local CBS station, so she was gone from about 4:30 to 8:00 in the morning. My dad was there, so it was safe to go back to sleep. I remember taking a photo with Mom and Elizabeth on a swing in the backyard when I was a legit baby, my dad crouching in front of us to take this lovely, idyllic picture. It can be nice remembering emotion-evoking memories from such early days, but it's also a challenge when trying to move past things that hurt. This tension is a big part of my life.

When I was born, my mom was a young television personality trying to find her way. By the time my memories started to form, she was a Charlotte star. I never knew anything otherwise, even when people asked me if it was weird that she was on TV. I only knew her as the mom who was present at every possible moment in spite of her busy career. She was brilliant with sewing and crafts. She was creative and patient in teaching me everything I wanted to know, and she could plan a party like nobody else. With our birthdays so close, Elizabeth and I shared bounce houses on more than one occasion. And not one of those janky, flimsy ones—I'm talking about one of those you see at the county fair that can hold ten normal-sized kids or seven fat kids.

She was a homemaker and a professional, a rarity in our neighborhood at the time, and she made it work. She was there when we needed her, whether to fix a boo-boo, congratulate us for an accomplishment big or small, or make us matching outfits for the first day of school. She was our biggest cheerleader and always made it clear that we were her top priorities in her life, even if it meant sacrificing her career.

The era of matching
expressions and
homemade outfits

Mom encouraged Elizabeth and me to explore arts and culture, but in a controlled way. *Silver Spoons*, *Family Ties*, and *Diff'rent Strokes* were our family favorites. Of course, my dad and I requested *The Dukes of Hazzard* and *Knight Rider*. Those were for the boys. We were free to watch age-appropriate programming, and since remotes were not yet universal and we weren't tall enough to control the knobs, the censoring was well controlled. The VCR, which sat too high atop the shelf on the built-ins, must have had a tape of *Grease* stuck in it. We watched that movie almost daily, but it was the version without the "Greased Lightning" part that stunned me at a later age. I had no idea what kind of magnet Danny claimed that car was.

Our dad, Clyde, was an old-school southern gentleman with an impressive resume, social demeanor, and jogging gait. He and our mom grew up in the same small town of Shelby, North Carolina. They both went to The University of North Carolina, married before he enlisted in the Navy, and then returned to Chapel Hill, where my dad earned his MBA. To start their life and family together, they moved to the big city of Charlotte, where he worked for the growing hometown bank. His employer, NCNB, turned out to be a large part of his story and his life, just as another company would be for me thirty years later.

Daddy of that era was a prototypical father, straight from Central Casting in all the best ways. During the week, it was gray suits and unmemorable ties with a leather briefcase in hand. On the weekends, it was Lacoste shirts, Duck Head shorts, white socks, and penny loafers. That was his outfit whether pushing a stroller, a grocery cart, or a lawn mower. Coors Light cans were never far from his hand. He had a dad bod before it was cool. He was funny, generous, and a little intimidating in the healthiest way. We had parents who spanked, and Elizabeth and I were better for it. He was the chief enforcer. When I exerted a tad too much independence and sass and received a well-earned disciplining, there were always safe arms waiting when I was ready to admit I was being a turd.

Our dad liked having us around for his rituals. Elizabeth and I would hop into his two-seat Fiat (car seat laws at the time were only suggestions) for weekly Krispy Kreme runs to procure our favorite donuts. On his nightly jogs, I was the Goose to his Maverick, except I piloted a bike since I could only run about the length of the driveway. This would remain the case for many years. Even things that weren't fun at all were made exciting when I was with my dad. He was a DIY-er who loved to take yard waste and other unknown materials to the landfill. I was fascinated by this wonderland of trash, dirt, and front-end loaders, and my dad was cooler than yours for bringing me to such a place.

I invited myself on every outing possible in that Fiat. It was the tiniest, sexiest, and least safe car available to the young professional dad of the time. Both the steering wheel and the stick shift knob were clad in smooth and shiny wood. The convertible top was extremely manual and cumbersome while being minimally protective against the elements. The dashboard had about six buttons and knobs, one of which fortunately controlled the radio volume. I was very good at turning it to the right. My dad loved roadhouse country and classic rock. The Oak Ridge Boys, Hank Williams Jr., and Bob Seger were mainstays. Occasionally I was given agency over the entertainment, especially when 107.9 WBCY spun "Dancing in the Dark" by Bruce Springsteen. I knew every word of that song and understood none of them. One afternoon, we stopped at the Record Bar on Providence Road so he could buy me the *Born in the U.S.A.* tape, allowing me to play Boss hits on demand. That purchase planted a seed that would blossom like kudzu many years later.

My dad's defining moment, the first highlight featured in his Dad Hall of Fame induction, was a project request that I mentioned in passing at age five. A favorite pastime among my neighborhood was to hunker down in ramshackle treehouses and "forts" made of wood scraps, old tables, and whatever treasured fortifications we could acquire. We would plan wars against nonexistent enemies, drop fuzzy knowledge about teenagers and what we heard they did, and outright lie about any personal conquests we had (not) achieved in recent days.

I mentioned that I wanted one of these bases in our yard. Daddy was on it. He went from zero to Bob Vila in one weekend. Over the next several weeks, we took almost daily trips to Lowe's to gather concrete for the foundation, posts to provide strategic elevation, two-by-fours for the frame, insulation for extra comfort, windows, shingles, more wood, and lacquer. One weekday afternoon, he did a drive-by of my school playground while returning from a solo supply mission. He had the top down with long pieces of wood jutting into adjacent lanes (which was not his problem). All of my first-grade classmates and I ran to the chain-link fence next to the slide to hear construction updates and bask in the gravitas of my dad. I could not have felt cooler if he was Robert Palmer himself.

In the end, he built an edifice that should have counted toward the square footage of the house. I'm pretty sure it was more temperature controlled than my own bedroom. It was high, huge, and pretty dangerous, but my dad built it with his bare hands without the help of Google. I still have the thin book purchased at Lowe's, which is more like a glorified magazine, that he used as a guide. I cherished that book for years.

Life for Elizabeth and me was simple, safe, and supportive. It was all we needed.

These memories share a common thread. None of them involved my mom and dad together. We were a textbook nuclear family who ate dinner together, attended church on Sundays, and vacationed to the beach in the summer. Elizabeth may have seen the seams popping. I didn't. I couldn't even put the pieces together that the fort was a project to keep him busy and out of the house.

One afternoon in 1986, my mom gathered nine-year-old Elizabeth and six-year-old me into my bedroom, the one with the Carolina blue ceiling and the painted clouds, to tell us that Mommy and Daddy were getting a divorce. She explained with great care that they loved us, they loved each other, and everything would be okay. I knew what a divorce was; I had heard of some kids whose parents lived in different houses. And ever since I'd learned that yellow and blue make green, I was pretty sure I knew everything there was to know about the world. When Mom asked us if we had any questions, Elizabeth bluntly asked, "Who will discipline us?" I asked about how helicopters work. True story.

We received a very similar debrief from my dad, but his speech was harder for me to take in. Something about his demeanor made me uneasy and sad. His voice communicated uncertainty. He promised that he would always be our dad and that he would be there for us. From the little I knew about divorce, dads were the ones who left, and moms were the ones in control. I knew that Mommy would be there for us all the time, but I didn't know where he would go. Maybe he'd move into the fort in the backyard.

In May of that year, Elizabeth and I walked home from school to a chaotic scene: furniture and cardboard boxes were piled in the front yard. It was moving day; my little brain could barely take in the great big moving truck with ramps, hand trucks, a really cool door on the side, and these big, strong guys who could carry a whole huge couch. This relocation wasn't a surprise to me, but I had no concept of what the process would look like. I remember walking upstairs to find that most of the furniture, including my awesome bunk bed, was gone. I went into my parents' room and saw a brightly colored spot on the carpet where a small sofa used to be. It was several shades bluer than the surrounding floor, shielded from the sun and twelve years of my parents' wear and tear. I remember finding long-lost LEGOs, almost a dollar in change, and errant Nilla Wafers that were once hiding beneath dressers.

The chaos of moving ultimately settled: my dad shifted into the Colony Apartments, and my mom, sister, and I moved into the outdated ranch at 3810 Ayscough Road. These locales were no more than a few miles from our old home at 811 Museum Drive, but we may as well have been on a far-off planet, like Greensboro or something. Elizabeth and I finished our last days at Eastover Elementary, a final cord that connected us to the lives we knew.

The impending summer would transition us into our new lives, new school, and new friends. We'd settle into our rec room, discover our creek, dive into an unfiltered exploration of popular culture, and become a support system for each of our parents, who were experiencing change that we couldn't understand. We were neither prepared nor qualified for the role.

CHAPTER 7

PAPER IN FIRE

All kids with summer birthdays get the short end of the stick, but the butt end of the stick is having a mid-August birthday, timed perfectly for every family's final summer vacation. Not only are you not in school to get properly celebrated, but your friends miss your parties.

My August 14 birthday was particularly painful in third grade when each student didn't just get a special day—they got an entire special week. During said week, a section of the bulletin board was dedicated solely to the special student's favorite things. At the end of the week, there was a little party with candy, crayons, and the creation of a birthday book for the kid in the spotlight. Each student drew a picture and wrote a message on a sheet of paper, and then Mrs. Bolt would staple it together and boom—a commemorative volume to keep forever or the next three days, whichever came first.

Thank goodness that Mrs. Bolt has a solution for the left-outs. She would assign each kid conceived in the fall a random week in the calendar without another classmate's birthday. Hence, a nondescript week in March 1988 became my "birthday." The aforementioned classroom bulletin board was slathered in North Carolina Tar Heels logos, hair metal posters, and, obviously, centerfolds of gaudy Italian supercars.

The latter was no surprise to anyone—I was allowed to keep a stack of car magazines on the corner of my desk for perusal once my work was done. This was the year I found out I was smart. I was always smart. I had taught myself how to read when I was three or four (scholars—aka my mom and my sister—argue the timing, but historians agree it was ahead of schedule and without assistance). I had never seen the benefits of being smart until the third grade, when it afforded me time to read the latest issue of *Automobile* magazine on school time. During elementary school, my teachers loved me for being smart, precocious, and responsible. I drove my teachers bonkers because while grades came easy, I worked consistently and diligently to make my classmates laugh. This was my early introduction to the thrill of attention and validation. Entertaining and engaging others would become a critical source of self-worth later in life.

At the end of my special week, I received my birthday book as was my third-grade constitutional right. I still have it. There were twenty-five students with twenty-five pages of bespoke drawings, messages, and scribbles targeted toward special me. Several of the pages said that I was "funny and weird." I can't think of two words that more accurately and pithily described me.

Funny and weird also described life for Elizabeth and me at the time. If not funny then fun, ever-changing, and a little confusing, but never bland. And weird? Weird is right.

We had settled into a life with our mom in the new house and our dad at his apartment. He would pick us up, take us on some of our familiar journeys and errands, and even let us swim in the pool at the divorced-dad apartment complex. And at home with our mom, things were fun. The three of us became a tight unit. Mom made our house feel whole, providing us with activities and letting us be kids without leashes. I don't remember hearing "no" very often; hence I went as Spuds MacKenzie for Halloween, complete with a can of Bud Light in my eight-year-old hand.

It was hard to understand at the time, but as an adult I get it now: you become accustomed to having a constant companion in your life. When your companion goes away, another tends to take their place faster than scripted. And when there are eligible bachelors and bachelorettes at the workplace—well, I guess that happens even faster.

My dad went first. He married Michele, his colleague at NCNB who was already a mainstay in Elizabeth's and my life. She was a regular passenger on the Boston Whaler Montauk 17 and the two-toned Carolina blue-and-white 1986 Chevrolet C10 regular-cab short-bed Silverado pickup, both of which my dad purchased post-divorce. He wasn't messing around with midlife-crisis baby steps; he went all-in on buying stuff he wasn't allowed to as a married man. Michele was materially younger than both of our parents, which was perfect for my dad, who was going through an epic rejuvenation. She was also the complete opposite of my mom in every conceivable way. Let's start here: Michele played Division I college basketball, and my mom unnecessarily went to the salon daily. Daddy and Michele married, and I was the best man. The main course at the reception was a pig pickin' (Google it, Northerners), and my dad got thrown into a swimming pool. All in all, a pretty good night.

My mom also jumped into a bathtub-sized dating pool and quickly married a coworker. From the files of you-can't-make-this-stuff up, she married the weatherman. Mike was *the* weatherman in Charlotte. In those days, the local forecaster in a tier-three city was a household name. It's a given to say it was bizarre to have this man we watched on the news climb out of the screen and into our house. That this character was a 50 percent Ron Burgundy anchorman presence, 30 percent Bill Walton tall hippie, and 20 percent John McEnroe temper-tantrum hothead made it cosmically disruptive. The man brought thirteen thousand vinyl records into our home. They married, and I was a non-defined male figure at the front of the ceremony. I blocked out the entire reception from my memory. I have no mental reel of it. That's rare for me.

In short order, yet another sea change occurred in Elizabeth's and my life. My father's employer was taking advantage of newly relaxed laws regarding interstate banking to buy distressed assets in Florida. As such, my father (being the reliable soldier he was) relocated with his new bride to Jacksonville, Florida. Elizabeth and I knew nothing of

Jacksonville, not even the ever-alluring smell of paper and coffee processing we'd soon experience.

Our evolving childhood family ecosystem was already in a precarious stasis before the Sunshine State news. On a scale of localized monster outbreak in *Gremlins* to full-on *Deep Impact/Armageddon* asteroid-level global disaster, we believed this was the La Brea tar pits erupting and becoming an active volcano in *Volcano* (not *Dante's Peak*). Most of those movies didn't exist yet, but you get the idea.

Elizabeth and I had discussed the divorce in the rec room and made a pros and cons list (there was no question she'd become an educational administrator and I'd become a management consultant). We knew it was a big deal; it would create some drama, but it was ultimately a situation to which we could adapt. Our final verdict was that this could be pretty rad. We had no idea how not-rad this new era would be.

On the afternoon they left for Jacksonville, Daddy and Michele came to our house to say goodbye. I vividly remember the truck and boat that we loved parked in front of our house. Michele deferentially stayed behind in the passenger seat while Daddy came inside to say farewell. He walked into the house and turned ten steps to the right, onto the pinkish-beige carpet in front of my bedroom door. We exchanged a few words I don't remember. Then he held Elizabeth and me in a three-way hug. His arms were wrapped around our little seven- and ten-year-old bodies, while his six-foot-one frame bent at the waist to bring his head closer to ours. It was silent. I was so sad and unsure, and I didn't know what to say. Elizabeth said nothing. I don't know how she felt. We stayed in that silent pose for what seemed like an hour.

A loud whimper and heave broke the stillness. I didn't recognize the sound. I thought maybe it was Daddy laughing. I was confused and startled. It happened a couple more times but louder and with a tighter grip on the two of us. The sounds were desperate and hurried. It was like he was being attacked. The whole thing lasted maybe ten seconds. Never before or since have I felt more pain, stress, and sadness emanate out of a human.

It was the first of two times ever in my life I saw my dad cry. It would have been less shocking to see his skin turn purple like the Smurfs in that one crazy episode than to see him cry. My dad, the tallest and second-strongest man I knew (behind my grandfather), the supremely rational and unflappable parent, cried like I did when I lost a stuffed animal.

He pulled himself together, subtly wiped the tears, and promised he would see us in a little while (a promise kept). He walked out the door to the wheel of the truck, and with happy waves and a few honks of the horn, Daddy and Michele were off to their life in Florida.

In the course of a ten-minute drop-in, my dad deposited on me the most traumatic moment of my life. I can't imagine how hard it was for him, and I never asked. Immediately afterward, I played with LEGOs or something. Who knows. It was a Saturday, so I bet we ordered pizza or went to Chili's (special occasions only). In our family's typical fashion, I stopped chewing on the moment and choked it down my throat like stale gum that had nowhere else to go. And as every seven-year-old of that era knew, when you swallow gum, it stays in your system for seven years. That gum has stayed in my system for thirty-five years and counting.

Daddy and Michele were gone. Mike was in our house. His and my mom's careers were growing and requiring more travel to Los Angeles to interview Hollywood types. All of the adults were doing the best they could. Elizabeth and I were taking it in as fast as we could. There was a lot of weirdness, but we were loved. For the next five years, our world split into three parts: Florida, Shelby, and home.

Florida

When I become a dad, I'll always view my kids as low-paid labor. I learned this from my dad's genius move to give my sister and me each a quarter for every moving company sticker we peeled from the newly relocated furniture. I think I earned close to ten dollars that day.

Daddy and Michele were living their best lives as the new couple in town and at work. They had a three-bedroom brick home tucked into

River Road in Jacksonville. It looked like a normal neighborhood and home from the front, but the lot backed up to Marco Lake, a small cove off of the St. Johns River. At the edge of the yard was a brand-new boathouse storing our beloved Boston Whaler. At any time of day, they could pop the boat in the water and go. Manatees would swim up to the grass and look for vegetation. All in all, it was a magical world.

Elizabeth and I flew to Jacksonville for extended visits three or four times a year, usually in the summer, around Christmas, and during other school breaks. It was a top-down, carefree, Jimmy Buffett-soundtracked life, heavy on sightseeing and parks but light on parenting stuff. We were fine with that trade. My grades were good, and my basketball was acceptable; I was a fun kid who could hold my own with my dad's friends who came to the backyard parties.

In spite of our dashing appearances, our two-on-two basketball team name was The Ugly Elephants

The gaps between the Florida trips were tough, but Daddy worked hard to make it as painless for us as possible. In the first few years, it was an unusual day if I didn't talk to him on the phone. I'd get a weekly greeting card from him telling me about his Florida life and what we'd do when I visited and congratulating me on my straight As. Every six weeks or so, he would come to Charlotte for work and make a point to stay in a hotel near our home. Those nights were the coolest. On a school night—a *school night*—we would go to dinner at Village Tavern, swim in the hotel pool, and spend the night partying in the hotel room. Then he'd drive us to school the next day in a nondescript rental car.

A couple of years into their Florida stay, Daddy and Michele moved to Miami. This was 1988, peak *Miami Vice* era. I was absolutely thrilled to see this new life and expected nothing short of pink tees, linen suits, and white Testarossas. Unfortunately, Coral Gables had fewer drug wars and bearded undercover vice cops than I was expecting. Gone was the backyard boathouse, replaced with an extremely small yard dominated by a mango tree. We'd take turns pitching mangos and crushing them with a baseball bat. It was total silliness.

Florida meant there was no time for discipline or being a traditional dad. I've now heard the term "Disney Dad," which isn't quite accurate, but it's close. More like a boat dad. There wasn't much in the way of order, discipline, coaching, and wisdom sharing. But there were plenty of burgers on the grill and water ski sessions.

As the Florida era came to a close, the trips felt a bit more procedural and less special. This dynamic is inevitable and natural with anything new and exciting. In this case, there was almost a sense of mutual apathy underpinning the whole operation. Elizabeth and I each missed trips, and the visits became increasingly interrupted by teen angst, real life, and work (including ones related to an unfortunately timed bank merger during an entire trip, a merger that would create NationsBank, which ultimately would become Bank of America).

Added to the dimming of the trips from bright neon to dull earth tones were two growing kids experiencing some of the most formative years of human life. I went from seven to eleven, and Elizabeth aged from ten to fourteen. It's not surprising that a dad lost touch with the slow, invisible-to-the-eye evolution of his kids from 733 miles away. The phone calls became more infrequent, and the postcard cadence was a little laxer. He was doing the best he could in a really hard situation.

Even so, Florida times remain among the most cherished moments of my life, ones that I chose to remember when later-stage content wasn't as appealing. It's like how I think of *Family Matters*. It was really great in the pre-Stefan Urquelle era.

Shelby

I saw a lot of cool things when I was a kid. I spent time in a television studio when my mom took me to work. I saw the inside of a Lamborghini Countach at the car show. I even once saw a monster truck crush a school bus. But nothing topped what I saw every couple of Saturdays—the inside of an unlocked Coke machine. They're not as big a deal anymore, but Coke machines were a bright light for us juvenile moths. I never saw a Coke machine to which I didn't want to feed quarters. I loved to hear its rumble and the dispensation of twelve ounces of empty liquid calories.

The inside of the Coke machine was a crowded affair, full of dozens of aluminum grenades of every flavor from Coke to Tab to Sprite to Fanta. The safe within the vault, requiring yet another sacred key, was the reservoir that collected all of the quarters, dimes, and nickels. No paper money in this vintage machine. Only kings and queens could possibly have access to this sugary, jingling trove of riches.

Couldn't you just go to the grocery store and see all of these cans and even more? Hush yourself, ye nonbeliever. It hits different inside the machine. It's just not the same.

My access to this wonderland was part of a typical weekend at my grandparents' house. My mom's parents owned two laundromats in the small mill town of Shelby, North Carolina, about an hour west of our hometown of Charlotte. Like our dad, our grandparents used Elizabeth and me as free labor to collect the quarters from the washers, the dryers, and the supreme royal entity of all machines, the Coke machine. We would go washer to washer and dryer to dryer to collect the quarters and dump them in a white bucket. We'd take the white bucket to the house, sit on the green shag carpet, stack the quarters into fours, group five of those stacks together, and insert the silver sleeve into a brown paper roller to make a ten-dollar cylinder of riches. It was a calming, orderly, and productive activity.

Calming, orderly, and productive best describe life in Shelby. Every weekend there started the same way. We would eat Bojangles (Google it, Northerners) for dinner and watch the ABC Friday night lineup (before it was called TGIF). On Saturday morning, we'd complete our laundromat cash extraction and then lunch in uptown before choosing a book from the library in the afternoon. Saturday dinner was usually on the grill, and then we'd watch a movie before *The Golden Girls*. In the downtime, I'd choose a book from the prodigious collection on the shelf or maybe explore the attic filled with military relics and outdated clothing and décor. On Sunday, we churched, brunched at the Western Steer, and then headed for the drop point with my mom at Eastridge Mall in Gastonia.

My mom's parents weren't even twenty years old when she was born. With that relatively narrow age gap came a sense of them being second parents to Elizabeth and me, which, at the time, was needed more than I realized. My grandmother Dede (short for Edith; scholars maintain that Elizabeth came up with the name) was the picture of elegance and a fixture in the social community of Shelby. She hosted a bridge club and walked into the Cleveland County Country Club like Queen Elizabeth. She was always beautiful and dressed to impress. Athleisure was never an option. Even at night, she wore elegant gowns as we talked and she patiently watched our juvenile TV shows. She was always inquisitive and paid special attention to what we did. Kid you not, she even listened to *Appetite for Destruction* with me a few times. Her mind was open, and her heart was enormous.

Dede also tolerated no nonsense and was not to be crossed. She would put me in my place in a heartbeat if I talked back. She expected us to behave, to contribute, and to respect elders. She was equally fierce in her defense of those she loved. One time at the Eckerd drug store at the mall, I was accused of stealing. I was in the candy aisle and put my hands in my pockets in a way that understandably looked suspicious. Of course, I was terrified of getting into trouble, particularly in Shelby, where there was a different set of laws, so I was not guilty. When the manager confronted Dede and shakily uttered, "Ma'am, we believe your son stole some candy" (our relatively small age gap created mom/ grandmother confusion), I dramatically and defiantly turned my pockets inside out. Dede did not hold back. That manager lived to regret that moment. Dede talked about the incident proudly for years.

My grandfather, Archie, was like a second dad. Archie was a fixture of Shelby. If Boss Hogg of Hazzard County and George Bailey of Bedford Falls stepped into that particle-melding machine from *The Fly*, it would yield Archie. Everyone knew him in town and far beyond the Cleveland County limits. Everyone had a story. He was that guy.

The Archie I knew was a kind, generous, and funny man with a cul-de-sac bald head, a deep closet of plaid flannel, and an arm that could rip a tree limb off the trunk. The dude was tough. He was a war veteran, was a 1950s dad, and eventually became a general contractor. That's several layers of tough. He had a chair that was unquestionably his; I kept it warm for him before he came home. When he arrived, I'd vacate; he'd occupy and then would smoke a pipe while watching any number of intellectual television shows, perhaps *Hee Haw* or *Grand Ole Opry*. I would run, jump, and breathe through the pipe smoke to immerse myself in the smell I loved so much. This carefree activity was acceptable because it was the 1980s, and secondhand smoke wasn't dangerous yet.

Archie took me along with him on adventures. I was his buddy. We'd ride around Shelby in his gigantic 1983 Cadillac Sedan DeVille with a CB radio, whip antenna, and trunk full (like absolutely jammed full) of tools. He taught me the etiquette of the citizens' band, which in turn taught me several lewd phrases and words spoken by nearby truckers. We'd go to "the shop," the epicenter of his contractor business that held his trove of tools and equipment. I would climb around front-end loaders, bulldozers, and large-scale cutting machinery with little oversight or care for personal safety. This unsupervised activity was acceptable because it was the 1980s, and sharp, rusted machinery wasn't dangerous yet.

Archie was always looking for deals, especially on things that neither he nor anyone on Earth needed. The best example that comes to mind was a cherry picker. You know, one of those trucks with a bucket attached to an arm that workers use to fix power lines and cut trees at towering heights. This wasn't just any cherry picker; this was his *eighth* cherry picker. His business had a need for roughly one cherry picker. With the surplus in hand, he was able to do extremely productive things like put me in the bucket and raise it to the maximum altitude while I yelled at people at street level.

If it wasn't obvious already, I loved and revered Archie. He was there to challenge me, keep me in line, and show me how to be a boy. He encouraged risks. It was safe because Archie would never let anything bad happen. He was Superman, if Superman was a small-town general contractor.

I loved being in Shelby. It was orderly, safe, and fun. I got discipline, adventures, and all the Nilla Wafers I wanted.

Home Doing the Best We Could

As with any day of the week, I generally had free reign over my television consumption on Sundays. Usually, this meant afternoon football on CBS. If I wasn't on my toes, the broadcast would end and give way to *60 Minutes*. To this day, the opening of a ticking clock and monotone host roll call gives me a hard pang of anxiety and a feeling of my heart dropping into my stomach. I'm a middle-aged man, a full grown-up. Yet still, the idea of Mike Wallace or Morley Safer announcing his name puts residual sadness and fear into my soul. When my weekends were over in fifth grade, I transformed into a tangled mess of irrational anxiety.

Life at home was odd. In just twenty-four months, we went from our carefree, idyllic life to tiptoeing around our own house. Our stepdad was unpredictably moody, and you never knew what might set him off. Given that we barely knew him when he moved into our home, we were not seasoned enough to know when his outbursts were coming. There was always tension hanging over a family meal, holiday, or night out—all of which became increasingly less frequent. The last "family" trip I can remember among the four people who lived in that house was shortly after Bush 41's inauguration.

Elizabeth and I initially coped with these changes in unique ways. Our afternoon creek explorations and roof hangouts gained dimensions of escapism. We began adding incremental make-believe elements to our existence. Sometimes we were twins. Sometimes our parents were famous people. We made up lives that weren't those of superheroes or characters we saw on TV. Instead, we simply created an everyday world in which we could temporarily find relief from a new world at home that wasn't suiting us.

The constant was our mom. She was doing the best she could to help us through all the change. She never let us feel deprioritized, even as she was building a new marriage. She gave us all of the opportunities and adventures she possibly could. Even as her (and our stepdad's) television career was in its prime, she made demands to be home in the afternoons to be there for us when we walked in from school. She and I had a particularly fun time when Elizabeth would spend the night out, and she always found something unique for us to do that was all about me.

Elizabeth began spending the night out a lot. While I was still in the little-boy phase of life, wanting only to ride bikes and walk the creek, Elizabeth was becoming a teenager with a burgeoning social life. She was a cool kid. She always was, which offered me a degree of social status even as a third grader. Being recognized by sixth graders made me playground royalty.

When she moved up to junior high, I was alone. When she spent more time out of the house, I was more alone. I lost my built-in buddy. I felt dreadfully lonely.

It didn't help that we moved yet again. Nor did it help that local television was changing in those days, leaving my mom and my stepdad behind. With Elizabeth exploring her life as a young adult and my stepfather becoming unreliable and volatile, my mom looked to me for emotional support. I was eleven years old and obviously unequipped to handle such things. I did the best I could.

While we had Florida and the semi-regular hotel staycation nights during my dad's visits to Charlotte, I felt an increasing sense of disconnection from my dad and all that came from it. I wasn't getting the same encouragement and healthy pushing to do boy stuff. Other kids' dads were little league coaches, handymen, and general male role models around the house. My friends were huntin', fishin', and lovin' every day. I was tagging along with my mom to the hair salon, grocery store, and makeup aisle at Belk's. I missed out on some of this development and, with it, a feeling of burgeoning manliness and the security of having a dad around.

Oversized sweater,
undersized confidence

When I was around ten or eleven years old, the other kids—particularly ones who were older, bigger, and cooler than me—began to notice my vulnerability. One afternoon at the pool, a thirteen-year-old kid bigger than us began violently throwing my buddies in the air and into the water. I knew he was coming for me next, so I got out of the pool and hid in the bathroom. This was the last time I ever got out of that pool. After going all day, every day during the summer to see my friends and live carefree days, I never returned. I would have been maimed, maybe even dead from drowning. And worse yet, humiliated in front of everyone.

School was no different. A few bullies zeroed in on me as an easy target—a weak kid whose dad hadn't taught him self-defense and wasn't there to protect him. They made it their mission to make life miserable for me, whether at school or in the neighborhood. They spent their days calculating ways to psychologically and physically torment me. It was their personal goal; I was all they thought about as they conspired new ways to keep me under their power. This went on during all of fifth and sixth grade. Because they were in my circle of friends, I withdrew and lost my neighborhood crew. It wasn't worth keeping my best friends if the price was pain and embarrassment from their lousy outer circle.

To make matters worse, I was about to go to junior high. The school that awaited me was much like Eastside High from *Lean on Me*, but there was no Joe Clark to protect me from the gang members and drug dealers. There was an active chapter of Cobra Kai at Alexander Graham Junior High, and they were ready to pick up from where my elementary school tormentors left me. With only me to protect myself, there was no way I was going to survive, let alone academically thrive to reach the potential and expectations placed on me.

This was also a time when the outside world had become extremely dangerous. In only eight years, I would be an adult. After going to New York with my mom and Elizabeth over the summer, I knew what awaited me—a life no different from Josh Baskin's when he became Big and had to move to the city. He was alone and helpless, and he had no resources—just as I would be. Even walking alone in Charlotte was dangerous. Being inside, behind closed doors, was the best bet for safety and a fulfilled life.

Of course, none of this was true.

The kid at the pool was playing a game with my friends who loved being tossed a few feet in the air, each of them lining up for another turn. The insecure kids at school and in the neighborhood were my friends expressing themselves in the only brutish way some kids know—by dishing out adolescent ribbing, which all boys do to each other. The junior high next door was obviously not the setting of *Dangerous Minds*. None of these rational facts soothed the intense worry and fear that gripped me. I saw what my brain wanted me to see. My own mind became an inaccurate interpreter of reality.

It didn't help that I didn't sleep on a Sunday night for the entirety of fifth and sixth grade. Every Sunday, when *In Living Color* would go to credits, I would start to work myself up about the mere idea of going to sleep and the terror of waking up for school. As anyone with Sunday Scaries knows, this is a vicious cycle of not sleeping, worrying about not sleeping, and therefore ensuring no sleep.

My mom knew something was wrong. My dad had to be told something was wrong. Nobody knew what to do. How could they know, when I didn't know how to communicate it? How could they help me when I was so scared of what they would think of me, what they would do to me, or what color my straitjacket would be in the padded-walled room at the mental institution?

I felt like there was no way out. I didn't know how to turn things around. My mind would go to increasingly fantastical forms of escapism. Disappearance, transformation, and grandiose "I'll show you" fantasies ruled my imagination. Rather than take steps to accomplish anything productive, I simply spiraled. The delusion was bordering on hallucinogenic—I would see people I feared in places where they weren't. There were lost hours in school from my mind going elsewhere for a few classes, thinking about all of the nonexistent threats that awaited me at every turn. There was simply no convincing me, as much as my mom tried, that everything was okay because, for me, it wasn't even close to okay.

Regrettably, I would only learn far later in life that what was happening was a product of both a physiological issue with my brain chemistry (serotonin reuptake and whatnot, things to which an actual doctor and not an amateur author should speak) and the situational context of my family. In short, the insecurity I felt at home, given my split family and a dash of chaos, generated a sense of being unsafe. My brain chemistry problems magnified, distorted, and remixed my responses to stimuli, to the point where I was not navigating the world in a rational manner. Had someone explained this to me back then, it would have saved a lot of mess later. But back then, we just didn't talk about these things.

This unchecked descent took an incalculable toll. I lost my friends. I stopped doing activities I loved. Trips to the mall, Hornets games, and even church sparked anxiety that I might run across a perceived enemy. Fear and paranoia stymied my concentration and cognitive processing ability. Said another way, I got dumb to the point that I had to repeat sixth grade.

As if the cards I was dealt weren't bad enough, I got fat. Food became an escape, and video games replaced goofing around and playing pickup sports. Getting fat further reduced my confidence and added to the mental strain. You could say that it was a cycle: I felt anxiety, fear, and self-loathing. I ate junk food to soothe those negative bugs in my head. I got fatter and felt even less confident. I ate to ease that feeling. Round and round we went in a pattern I'd mirror in a different way later in life. I didn't realize that by eleven years old, the table was set. The seeds were planted. The cards were dealt. The twenty-sided die was cast. The game was afoot. My physiological brain chemistry, coupled with the experiences that I had as a little kid, set the course for the next few decades. The once-innocent escapism of youth became dangerous, selfish, and nearly irreversible behaviors thirty-one years later.

CHAPTER 8

HOLDING BACK THE YEARS

In my first sixteen years, I knew that the worst-case scenario of any situation could conceivably happen, but I had never seen it actually occur. That was until June 19, 1996, my first day of work (defined by a boss, a time card, and a paycheck into which the taxman dipped his cup). It was no surprise to my family that I sought to work in a car dealership, as I had been obsessed with cars from an early age. I went from Tonka trucks to Micro Machines to hand-built models until I could finally drive real ones. Once I got a taste, I wanted more—I wanted to drive every car I could get my hands on. Since age sixteen was when my sister and I were required to get out of the house and work, where better than a car dealership? (According to Elizabeth, Banana Republic. Her family discount on trendy button-downs was more useful than my invoice plus $200 deal on Camaros.)

I reported for duty at City Chevrolet, Charlotte's largest Chevy dealership and one of Cole Trickle's sponsors in *Days of Thunder* (before he got the Mello Yello deal and sparked a rivalry with Rowdy Burns). My job was naturally at the bottom of the food chain—the service porter. That's the guy who puts the plastic on your seat and the paper on the floor mat when you pull your car into the service lane. We service porters would park and retrieve cars, jump-start the dead ones (1987 Camaros tend to have this issue), and keep the department clean. I took particular pride in maintaining a service lane devoid of any liquids and clear of debris. That floor was my jurisdiction, my domain, and no coolant or oil could withstand my mop.

It was a sweaty, smelly, and rather gross job, particularly when we needed to move a hoarder's car that had sat in the 95-degree Carolina sun for a few hours. I couldn't be happier. This was the first step in making it big in the automotive retail industry. I wanted to be the next Rick Hendrick (non-Southerners or car people, Google him), who happened to be a close friend of the family and who set me up with the job. By putting in my time at the bottom, I would learn the ins and outs of the operation, giving me the credibility to one day be a dealership baron.

Over the next six years of high school and college, I worked at five dealerships. My last role was selling Hondas. There's an entirely separate book full of lessons and stories from that. But that's not what we're here for. We're here to talk about that first job at City, the one that would teach me all I needed to know to be successful in the professional world.

Hustle Matters

My peers and managers knew how I got that job and that I was being paid a princely sum of $6 per hour. I was not necessary; the boss got me there, and I was costing hundreds of dollars to the multimillion-dollar operation. In my mind, that meant I had to work twice as hard as everyone to earn my keep. I ran from place to place. I never sat, and I never said no. One day, an influential mechanic (believe me when I tell you that there is a social hierarchy in a service department) stopped me in my tracks—a move that typically preceded a terse complaint or a barked command. Instead, he told me that I was the only one who hustled and he noticed it. He made my life easier for the rest of that summer. Word spread and, in the end, the head of the enormous service department congratulated me for proving him wrong. He'd expected me to be a lazy, entitled snot. That relentless need to earn my compensation never went away, even (and especially) when my income picked up a second comma.

Being a Jerk Gets You Nowhere

Among the mechanics and the service agents, there were nice people, and there were jerks. There were six service porters. We were cheap labor that helped the operation function. We had flexibility in which mechanics and agents we wanted to help—and invariably, we stuck to the ones who treated us well. In fact, we tended to ignore the jerks, which made them even jerkier, which made us even less likely to focus on them. Just because you're in a position of authority doesn't mean you have to be an authoritarian. Being nice matters.

When You Mess Up, You Own Up Straight Up

Back to that first day of work and worst-case scenarios. Clearly, the worst thing that could happen on the first day of work at a car dealership would be wrecking a car. Well, I managed to do that. A customer was picking up his windowless fifteen-passenger van (I did not see loose candy or any other kidnapper accessories), and I was there to perform retrieval duty. In the crowded service lot, I reversed the van using only the rear mirrors and blind hope instead of actually seeing what was in my way. The coast was clear until the protruding nose of a bright-red Saturn coupe made friends with the bumper of the vessel I was captaining.

After seeing the visible damage, I proceeded to panic, swear, sweat, and prepare for the end of my entire career. There was no way to escape, so I did what a rule-follower does and told the teacher (well, manager in this case) what I had done. I was terrified and awaited swift reprisal or perhaps a shameful permanent dismissal. Instead, I was met with gratitude for my honesty and assurance that "this stuff happens" (spoken in stronger service department parlance). Later in the summer, I saw the repercussions of a colleague not owning up to a mistake and instead trying to hide it. It did not turn out well. Since then, I've always come clean when a disaster strikes. There's no upside to hiding it.

These lessons have been three of the primary principles of my career thus far. They have served me well. In the end, I did not put these tenets into practice in the car-focused career of which I dreamed. Cars remain a passion and interest of mine, so much so that I use them as analogies to help me learn a number of topics. I have used car brands, parts, and driving techniques as ways to both teach and learn anything from hotel reservation economics to corporate information technology. Here, I will use a car analogy to explain what happened over the last thirty years that led me to my first morning in a mental institution.

Let's start with the assumption that in driving and in life, it's best to stay on a paved road that leads to a desired destination. No matter the destination, the best route utilizes asphalt. Or, as Tom Cochrane said, life is a highway. I didn't want to say it, but I know you were thinking it. And I'm not proud of how basic this part of the analogy is, but stay with me.

My delusional, irrational, and life-darkening meltdown when I was eleven made it clear that something in my mind didn't compute reality and couldn't consistently muster rational thinking. I could not rely on my brain to recognize and interpret hazards ahead, and I didn't trust myself to navigate these dangers nimbly and deftly. I was known, instead, to veer all the way off the road to avoid troubles. In this sense, I was born a car with bad steering.

Even with bad steering, I was able to stay on the road in my early childhood. I had two parents who provided safety and guidance. They instilled values, beliefs, and reward/punishment systems that kept me on a narrow path, even when I tried to zag. My grandparents, teachers, and healthy role models also pushed me back to where I needed to be. In that sense, I had sturdy guardrails in place.

At age seven, my life was upended in a year's time. My parents divorced, and we moved to a new neighborhood and school. We had new stepparents. My dad moved to Florida (complete with the traumatic farewell), and life at home was . . . weird. Over the next few years, I lost Elizabeth to her social life, and I lost a link to my dad. My mom became more reliant on me for emotional support. In these senses, life took a sledgehammer to my guardrails and bent them out of shape.

With the guardrails out of shape, I flailed on the bumpy shoulders of the road; I lost my grip on reality and a path to a healthy future. I teetered on the brink of a full-on crash and burn at age eleven when I lost my friends, non-husky pants, and good grades.

I'm about to run through about fifteen years at breakneck speed. That's purposeful because honestly, my life isn't that interesting or unique. It was comfortable. I had privilege and opportunities. There is nothing exceptional about it. And that's the entire point—my uninteresting, unremarkable middle school, high school, college, and young adult years still led me to a psych ward. Movies and TV have misled us into thinking that severe traumas or unimaginable challenges are what lead to mental health challenges. That is not the case.

Middle School: Hitting the Reset Button on the Nintendo Console of Life

All of the early damage to the guardrails was not enough to break them. My guardians made a drastic move to shove me back onto the road: I changed schools and stayed back a grade. This effectively erased the context that had created so much undue fear and anxiety. I became the happy and bright kid who had disappeared years earlier. I quickly made friends and started what felt like a totally new life. And man, I was really, really good at sixth grade the second time around.

By the end of eighth grade and middle school, I was back on the smart kid path and well liked. I was robbed of victory in the prestigious annual speech, which, to this day, I believe was an injustice. That speech was seventh-grade genius, a funny and charming diatribe in response to the prompt of "why I want to be president of the United States." I lost that battle, but I received some level of consolation a month later when I won the election for middle school president. I was the lead in the school play and held the most powerful position on campus.

These accomplishments didn't move the needle much where I needed them to. In the same time period, my dad and Michele moved back to Charlotte after their five-year stint in Florida. This was theoretically a good thing, but in reality so much had changed. Elizabeth had her own life, and my dad didn't understand or empathize with the mental health complexities of mine. Their return was not the celebration that we had once believed it would be.

Their return was further complicated by them having two new kids, Jonathan and Courtney, in the first three years that they were back. Today, it's embarrassing and shameful to express exactly how gut-wrenching that development was for me and how it impacted me for the next decade and a half. I was already struggling to get the attention and affirmation I needed from my dad, and from that point on, the maximum possible volume of validation was diluted considerably. Regardless of how hard I tried and achieved, my dad would not communicate his pride directly to me. Instead, I witnessed ample praise going to the new kids. It never got better. The guardrails weakened.

At home, local television changed and left my mom and stepdad behind. The days of the powerful local news personality had passed in favor of extremely willing, low-cost replacements from Peoria aspiring to make it to Pittsburg. The station that my mom and stepdad loyally served for decades cut them. For them, it meant finding ways to adapt and survive. For me, it added another layer of insecurity at home, coupled with some heaping emotional support expectations. Elizabeth—for the most part already gone from my life as a busy, popular, high school cool girl—was on her way to Chapel Hill to attend the family school, The University of North Carolina. The guardrails weakened.

There I stood in the summer of 1994—a chunky kid who was ready to take the reins of his strange life and write his own story. I was low on confidence and high on aggrandized visions of financial, social, and romantic success in my home city of Charlotte. I was all-in on making the insecurities of my home life go away, proving to my dad that I was a worthy son who would make him slow clap at a variety of ceremonies, and earning the respect of my peers (particularly the female ones; I was fourteen, after all) by being an independent and unique character. These are tall tasks. The car's steering would need to be in fine shape.

High School: Camouflaged in an Insecurity Cloak

Nobody needs another long-winded memoir of high school in the 1990s—it is well covered in television and the movies. Instead, here's a series of haikus about those four years:

I was a good kid
No alcohol, no smoking
Too scared of trouble

Yes, I got good grades
But I was not ambitious
Could have done much more

I was insecure
Until I lost thirty pounds
And grew some inches

I gained confidence
Lifting weights and working out
And throwing discus

No dating for me
Girls loved me like a sister
Constantly friend zoned

I tried with my dad
I sought his validation
It was not working

Only one college
Received my application
Luckily, got in

Overdue justice
Take that, speech contest
I spoke at graduation

Guardrails guided me
Damaged, weak, and vulnerable
They would be tested

Michael Stutts: The College Years

One day, after my nineteenth birthday in August 1998, I checked into room 1812 in Granville Towers West, smack in the heart of Chapel Hill, North Carolina's lousiest shopping center. It was, however, one of the town's epicenters of frivolous undergraduate life at The University of North Carolina. I maintain that those of us who spent 1998 to 2002 in college experienced among the wildest series of changes that any cohort tucked into a university bubble could possibly experience. Hear me out:

Topic	Entering college	Exiting college
Cell phones	Only for use while being actively murdered	Ubiquitous, flip phones, must wait for nights and weekends
Music	Black canvas Case Logic CD holder, the thicker the better, burned CDs for crushes	Rise and fall of Napster, music stored on magical MP3 players
Terrorism	Not really a thing, mostly in *Die Hard* movies	Post-9/11 unity, "Proud to be an American" on repeat
Computers	Giant desktop with tank-sized CPU and/ or colorful iMac	Mandatory laptops, thick as an encyclopedia

Topic	Entering college	Exiting college
The internet	AOL CD-ROMs with 500 free hours over dial-up	High-speed ethernet cords, no interrupted phone calls
Radiohead	Guitars/bass/drums, some weird synth stuff	Weird synth stuff, some guitars/bass/drums
Lemonade	Country Time	Mike's Hard
Destiny's Child	Knowles, Rowland, Roberson, Luckett	Knowles, Rowland, Williams
European currency	A multitude of sovereign currencies	The euro, except in the UK, or England, or however that works
Stained blue dresses	Not a Halloween costume	Halloween costume
Corporate accounting	Boring, Arthur Andersen exists	Exciting thanks to Enron, Arthur Andersen no longer exists
Diets	Low fat, lots of bagels, no red meat	Low carb, bagels are the devil, red meat encouraged
Star Wars	Three movies, all fantastic and iconic	Five movies, one of which is total trash
New Orleans rap	No Limit	Cash Money
Mountain Dew	Only Diet and Regular	Regular, Diet, Code Red, Diet Code Red
Chads	Michael Murray, Lowe	Hanging, dimpled, pregnant
Street racing	Not really a thing	Hondas and Mitsubishis are considerably faster and more furious

My goals entering college were simple:

- Get good grades as a business major.
- Have a perfect level of fun—no regrets and no major trouble.
- Go to as many basketball and football games as possible.
- Set myself up for the rest of eternity with a stable job in Charlotte where I could raise a family with a beautiful sorority girl.

I got good grades. I had fun without major trouble and am extremely thankful that there were no cameras around. I went to lots of events, but UNC went through a lowly run of sports at the time.

An egregious, non-sequitur photo of the best costume of Halloween 2000 on Franklin Street (and possibly of all time)

As for the last goal—well, that one absolutely did not happen. It wasn't even close. Looking back on it, I didn't want or need any of those things at that stage in my life, and in many ways, it's a miracle that I didn't get them. These objectives were motivated not by a love for Charlotte, a deep intrinsic interest in how money flows through the banking system, or the lovely woman I was dating (she really is a great person, and we've kept in touch over the years). Instead, they were entirely inspired by the utopian, unrealistic, and unhealthy idea that if I could replicate my dad's life and career, then I would certainly earn the sense of validation from him that I sought. Better yet, if I could amp up each element by a degree or two, then I'd feel the love even more.

I was a college senior in the fall of 2001. September was when the financial institutions of New York City and beyond would fly a team of Brooks Brothers-suited representatives into Chapel Hill to make enormous promises of success and prestige in investment banking to impressionable and desperate twenty-one-year-olds. These sessions usually featured a handful of recent UNC graduates with business cards, substantial eye bags, and advice tinged with longing (on the order of "enjoy college while you can"). We could see the visible toll that the one-hundred-hour workweeks were taking, but still we jumped through every hoop imaginable for the honor of replacing these graduates when they completely burned out.

The eleventh of that month was a red-letter day, as three investment banking titans would be descending for a dog and pony show on campus. At 9:15 that morning, we stood stoically in the cafeteria, watching burning buildings in New York on television. We knew that everything about that day, month, year, and the foreseeable future would change. Obviously, those and many more investment banking sessions thereafter were canceled. Our fleeting career opportunities paled in comparison to what was happening.

I can remember most things about that day and the order in which they happened. It wasn't very different from the experiences of others. With that said, I bet I'm one of the few who joined his friends to watch *Joe Dirt* to take our eyeballs and minds off of what was happening on television. It did not work. As soon as it was off, it was back to the constant crawl of death tolls and hearsay on the bottom of the screen. The radio stations, regardless of format, were all playing news or "God Bless the U.S.A." for several days. That day changed the tone of a lot of lives. I still don't feel like I did enough to serve or react.

We carried on. We interviewed for our post-graduate jobs, and I managed to secure a place at a competing bank to the one at which my father had spent the last thirty years. Not for lack of trying to go to his—I interviewed and was promptly rejected for two different roles. There is no question that this was for the best. Luckily, there were enough forces in the banking recruiting universe to counter my ill-aimed ambitions.

Welcome to Atlanta

In August 2002, I made the move to Atlanta, along with several UNC friends. The nice girl I was dating at the time moved there as well. In less than a year, it was predictably over for us. I had swung and missed on my big move to be like my dad out of the gates. I chalked it up to circumstance, to limited job options because of geopolitical market shocks, and to bad fortune. I still felt like I was in a position to receive some positive reinforcement if I played things right.

I was good at my job. I had quick success by employing one of my City Chevrolet principles: work harder than everyone else, no matter the task. My first assignment as an investment banking analyst was not to run a complicated discounted cash flow model or to evaluate competitive pricing on recent capital markets transactions, both of which my education prepared me for. Instead, I was asked to find every document, printed and electronic, related to Enron that we had on file. I made copies, boxed them, and shipped them to the government. It felt a lot like Robin Williams in *Mrs. Doubtfire* when he walked into the film warehouse and asked if he would be introducing movies on camera but was instead told to box and ship them.

My copying, boxing, and shipping process was so thorough and efficient that word got around that I was a fantastic analyst. At the time, I found this quite odd and worrisome. My friends were buried deep in Excel while I was slaving all day and night over a hot Konica copier. That's when I learned how being industrious *and* humble mattered. Later in my career, I would ask junior new hires to do some fairly strange tasks (e.g., go to every location of a particular fast-food restaurant in an entire metropolitan area and take a picture of the menu) and quickly evaluate their potential based on their reactions. "I went to Harvard" does not get one out of paying their dues.

For three years, I faced every opportunity and obstacle of a typical early-twenties college grad. New relationships, job opportunities, and drifting away from college friends were inevitable. Elizabeth proved to be a strong guardrail at the time. She and I had grown apart over a ten-year span between her high school years and our college years. As she entered real life in her move to Atlanta, she began reaching out to me more. I was happy to have her back. Her presence in Atlanta was comforting as I started my adult life and career.

Elizabeth had found her permanent footing in Atlanta. She began dating and eventually married a mostly reformed frat dog (said in the most loving and respectful way). Brett and Elizabeth had their first of three children shortly after my move there. They built a home together (figuratively at first, then literally), melded their social and family lives in a maddeningly perfect and functional way, and founded their relationship around Jesus and the Bible.

Elizabeth's guardrails were equally broken in many of the same ways as mine. She had some of her own experiences that are very painful and hers to share. She is blessed to have been able to repair, strengthen, and build new guardrails that have held her on course to this day.

I held on to whatever guardrails I could. I walked through the motions at church with Elizabeth and her family. I drove to Charlotte about once a month. I worked and worked to be the best banker I could be and show my dad how well I had turned out. None of it worked, and one more hit to my guardrails would finally break them wide open. The Michael-with-a-lit-torch-and-can-of-gasoline era would soon begin.

CHAPTER 9

THE FINAL COUNTDOWN

Neurological intensive care units (NICUs) have strict rules. For twenty minutes about every six hours, patients' family members can join their loved ones' bedsides to have caring conversations. Support teams would gather in the waiting room about fifteen minutes before the doors opened. For those who haven't been part of this bummer of a ritual, the room is stale, beige, itchy, and quiet, save for the occasional muffled conversation or sob. The sole form of distraction is a TV, usually showing some nonthreatening network content or maybe some racy HGTV or Food Network fare.

In the prime-time hours of September 2005, there was only one option on the sad room television: *Deal or No Deal*. As a reminder, this prolific game show featured a bald germaphobe goading average Americans to defy basic laws of probability in an attempt to outwit a faceless banker by capturing money held in one of twenty-six metal briefcases under the protection of agency models. It was pretty much the best show ever. One night in particular, there were about fifteen visitors, including me, waiting to enter the NICU when a critical briefcase opening was nigh. This show was so riveting that many of those fifteen people sacrificed three of their precious twenty minutes to bridge the commercial break and witness the "open the case" moment. NBC could have morbidly twisted that fact into a promotional nugget.

Two months earlier, there were no NICU visits or tense briefcase openings on my agenda. In July 2005, I was established in Atlanta, both in my job and in my social life. I was on a comfortable and successful track. I had a blue Honda Accord with 180,000 miles and lived in an outdated ranch house with four dudes. We had one of those big-screen TVs the size of a VW Beetle airing mostly sports and *South Park*. My mid-twenties life was pretty great, and the forecast called for mostly sunny with a chance of strong to quite strong.

That all changed with a phone call I received while driving to the Atlanta airport. I was on my way to meet my girlfriend's family at their lake cottage in Michigan for the Fourth of July. My tiny little flip phone rang, and in a pre-texting and pre-Bluetooth era, the only real option was to answer while driving. It was my dad, so I felt compelled to answer rather than operate a motor vehicle safely. I was still going through all the effort to impress him with my career and life in general, but our communication was slipping quickly. My visits home waned, and our phone call frequency dropped to about once every two or three weeks. When he called, I always answered.

We small-talked about work, the stock market, my upcoming trip, who knows. Then he changed his tone into one I hadn't heard since I was seven years old. He became very serious, his voice changing octaves, and he took control of the conversation. I could tell he had something important to say because he always became really awkward when sharing big news. He explained that he was having trouble using his right hand. Writing, typing, and everyday activities like cranking a car or operating a chainsaw had become nearly impossible. He told me about all of the physical therapists and hand specialists who couldn't find an issue. He even thought he had carpal tunnel syndrome. He recounted how one of these doctors finally referred him to a neurosurgeon who saw something "funny" in a scan of the left side of his brain that controlled his right-side functionality. He told me not to worry and to have fun with Molly's family, tell her hello, and be careful. We had long ago mastered a way of getting off the phone in a way that replicated a formal handshake. Onward I flew to Walloon Lake for fireworks and fun.

I had a sinking feeling that his life was coming to an end and mine was about to change. He wouldn't have told me anything if he didn't know it was very bad.

Over the next two months, there were more scans, more mass visible on said scans, surgery plans, and zero good news. The ramp-up culminated in Labor Day weekend brain surgery to extract as much of the rapidly organizing and growing tumor as possible. We waited for a report, hopeful that the surgery would resolve the problem and we could move on. I even hoped for a new relationship with him once he'd had a brush with mortality.

That didn't happen. You know that moment toward the end of *The Perfect Storm*, when *Andrea Gail* and her crew are being thrown around by waves? They survive a big one and then see the monster ginormous wave that they couldn't have seen until it was coming right for them. Well, this was the neurosurgical cancerous mass extraction version of that. The tumor was much larger than they expected. It had grown quickly, and it was corkscrewing into his brain. The early reads were a death sentence. Morale was low among everyone. For a few days, we cycled between the waiting room, the NICU, and *Deal or No Deal*.

The final diagnosis came a few weeks later. On Sunday, September 25, 2005, I was standing in a blazing-hot Zilker Park in Austin, Texas. The sky was cloudless, and the sun was angry. The drought-suffering lawn was more like a middle school softball infield. That weekend, I risked heat exhaustion and hipster overload to attend the Austin City Limits Music Festival. The biggest-font acts of that year's lineup were Oasis and Coldplay, a fascinating collision of two British bands hurtling in opposite trajectories, intersecting at the midpoint of main-stage relevance. Self-importance, bombast, and brotherly rivalry were entertaining enough, though neither band compelled me to burn my skin three layers deep.

The prevailing motivator for my sunburn was Arcade Fire, a bizarre freight train of instrument-swapping musical outcasts who had taken over the "indie rock" (the stupidest genre name ever) scene. In 2005, they were listed in the second-smallest font on the third line of the festival poster, slotted for a fifty-minute afternoon set on the second-largest stage of the festival grounds, and ultimately captured the largest crowd of the weekend as *the* band to see. Six years later, they were the top-of-the-poster headliner of the same festival.

I approached the stage about thirty minutes before the scheduled set time. One must be patient and accept boredom/people watching/absurd conversation eavesdropping if one is to gain advantageous sight lines at a massive festival. About ten minutes before showtime, my tiny mobile flip phone rang. It was my aunt, my father's sister, telling me that my dad wanted to talk to me. Unable to find an open, quiet space, I instead got low to the dusty, occasionally grassy ground. I took a knee to avoid the din of the crowd, doing that thing where you contort the side of your face closest to the phone and plug your opposite ear, as if that's going to make you hear better. I could hear most of what my dad said. In choppy sentences and in a broken voice, he told me that his cancer was officially terminal and that he was on a timeline. As usual, we did our handshake conversation ending, but this time I told him I loved him and would see him soon.

I won't belabor the next eight months. Suffice it to say that in the early stages of the death sentence, I poured every bit of myself into making the most of the remaining time. I imagined a total reconciliation and resolution of all open threads between us, culminating in a freeze-frame hug before the closing credits. All of the missed (mediocrely performed) sports events, father-son skills training, and lifetime wisdom would be injected straight into my veins through a wide-gauge needle of terminal illness urgency.

I temporarily moved to Charlotte, made myself available to help around his house, and spent much of my free time at his side. We had a few starts and stops of important conversations, but my hopes were never fully met. I realized that my fantasy was just that, and slowly I began to seep back into my Atlanta life. I was sad and defeated. I was unsettled knowing that there was a ticking clock. I didn't trust how his eventual death would hit me emotionally. I had cried only once in the whole process, and I assumed that something explosive was brewing underneath.

On Wednesday, May 17, I was at my office in Atlanta when my stepmother, Michele, called to reel me home to Charlotte. The end was imminent. On the previous Sunday, I had been at their home. Everything had seemed stable. I thought there would be a little more time, at least enough to come home for another visit. As was typical for a Sunday afternoon drop-in, I was in a hurry to get on the road by 3:00 p.m. in order to make it to Atlanta for dinner with friends. I remember so clearly my dad asking me if I could stay a little longer. He had never asked me to do that before. And instead of a handshake, he asked for a hug. He must have known something I didn't.

I got to his house early that Wednesday evening. I tried to bring the sunshine as I shuffled to his bedside. I knew that his blinds were shut for good. I had a few moments alone with him to tell him I loved him and that I would make him proud. I would carry the Stutts name. I asked him to look out for me. I told him I hoped I had already made him proud. If I could've asked him whether I had, I don't know if I would've had the courage.

Elizabeth arrived shortly after I did. She had her little newborn son Reid with her. I took a photo of his tiny hand in my father's withered, scarred, and unrecognizable hand. It's the only picture of them together.

It took a few days for the end to come. At about midnight on Friday night, I went to his house to sleep and to be an extra adult in the house. My little brother and sister, fifteen and twelve, were asleep in their rooms. I slept in the guest room. Two hours later, early on May 20, Michele woke me up. He was gone. I was relieved it was over.

We buried him on a Tuesday, I think. I spoke at the funeral. People seemed to like it. Once again, I proved the seventh-grade speech contest judges wrong. I really should have won. Maybe losing was the motivation I needed to hold court so effectively at my father's funeral. If true, that's a seriously long game.

Two days later, I left for a bachelor party. A week after that, I left the United States for the first time. Three months later, I moved to Chicago to start grad school. I had options closer to home, but the school I chose was far away and would take me further than I ever imagined.

The last bolt holding the fragile guardrails had popped. Off I went for the next sixteen years, barreling off road like one of those Baja trucks that bounces off sand and rocks in the desert. Except in my case, I forgot the GPS and a good set of shock absorbers.

III.

Just Like Heaven

CHAPTER 10

THE WAY IT IS

T he first few days on the unit are largely defined by the shock of
deprivation. People, places, technologies, habits, freedoms, prefer-
ences, and compulsions are taken away all at once. In the days leading
up to my entry, I was cripplingly overwhelmed about this idea. But once
you face it, there's really nothing to it. There's great comfort in being
bereft of choices and options, as long as you submit to the loss of control
(which not everybody did, or at least not at first). It was hard to watch
some of the newcomers resist the reality that this was their home. Some
of them took it out on the staff. I really didn't like that.

With that said, it is extremely difficult to not be able to move around
as you wish. The vast majority of our activity was contained within the
walls of the unit, which pretty much consisted of four rooms. This is
why even when we were not hungry or itching to work out, we would
go to the cafeteria or gym just to get outside and activate our bodies.
Weight gain is easy when you're sedentary and mainlining soft serve.
As if the threat of getting fat wasn't bad enough, I had to also consider
that I would be pasty white. I loved being outside in my Florida life. I
was proud of my well-defined farmer's tan. It was gone three weeks in.

If you wanted or needed to go outside the unit, you had to find a staff
member who could open the door and chaperone you. It wasn't until
three weeks into my stay that I earned the right to walk alone around

the courtyard, but even then, I had to ask permission and check in every fifteen minutes. In short, you just couldn't go where you wanted to. I went six weeks without turning a doorknob of my own volition. Not to worry; it's like riding a bike.

Journal entry: Wednesday, April 13, 2022

This is a hospital

This is a shock

I'm an inmate, a new kid, a broken toy

These aren't my people

I'm lost. I'm aimless

I'm comfortably numb

I've told the same story three times now

I'm exhausted

Low point: Going through my things. That sucked

Dinner alone = bad

Hornets got crushed. Bummer

Looking back on the words I wrote, so much of it is about how miserable I felt. That day felt fifty hours long, starting with my flight with Elizabeth and ending with the traumatic intake process and my first meetings with my new friends. Days earlier, I had circled the Charlotte Hornets playoff game as something that could act as a touch point for my real life. As a Charlotte kid, of course I am a Hornets fan, though I can't say I was a particularly loyal one by that point. That didn't matter—anything with some level of familiarity was an injection of warmth in a chilly new environment.

I spent a lot of that afternoon asking how to operate the television (a skill that would come in handy later on, as I was able to control the content we watched) so that I could ensure my basketball comfort blanket would be in place.

The Hornets lost 132 – 103. A real kick in the teeth to end a rocky day.

Journal entry: Friday, April 15, 2022

Sleeping well, kinda shocked

I don't know when to wake up

I still can't work out. It's driving me crazy

I got my new pillows and mattress topper. These feel nice

I also got my snacks. I like snacks

We had a pizza and ice cream party last night

I'm more depressed than anxious

We watched Smokey and the Bandit tonight

We ate outside

There are lasers keeping us in

This is crazy how am I here

I miss my life

But I need to be here

The second full day was when I gave in to my new home. I went from feeling sorry for myself and drifting through the motions to identifying ways to shape an environment in which I could thrive. That, of course, included junk food, proper sleeping accoutrement, and 1970s comedies with highly questionable dialogue. It was still an emotional EKG chart from hour to hour—it was disorienting to move from the lows (the facility's locked-down nature, the perimeter lasers, the workout shutdowns) to the highs (pizza, ice cream alfresco on the high-walled back patio). There was also a risk of not fitting into even my stretchiest athleisure.

My overriding sentiment was that there was no way this could be my story—locked in a place like this, the kind of thing you see on TV or hear about from the messed-up neighbors. It's not the kind of place that high achievers go, especially not voluntarily. Paradoxically, I was completely confident that I had made the right decision, as long as I blocked out the fear that my career and life would never recover.

Journal entry: Sunday, April 17, 2022 (Easter Sunday)

I loved today

So much time with the group

I'm tired of being the new guy

I like it here

It's like my fantasy of disappearing

A chance to be productive

And to binge watch a lot of TV

So many compulsive behaviors forbidden

Watched home church

Went to Easter service here

Felt good

These are my people for now

I'm happy

For now

It was so lovely

These are my people

I never would have guessed that by the end of my first weekend, I'd feel so safe, comfortable, and hopeful as I did. I didn't think I'd laugh or look forward to nights binge-watching Netflix on uncomfortable chairs.

Our cohort felt like misfits who'd found each other, and after the unique turmoil and traumas that brought us there, it was soothing and even joyous to have each other.

Obviously, it's a good thing to become comfortable in a new environment, especially one you'll be in for a long time. The downside is getting too accustomed to a completely unsustainable situation. Who wouldn't love being trapped in a place that prevented even the option of being real-world productive? Who couldn't get used to not having to talk to people they'd rather avoid? When had anyone ever turned down unlimited access to a soft-serve ice cream machine?

Before walking through the doors of the unit, I'd valued independence and freedom above most things in the world. At this place, there were strict rules, rigid order, and an unassailable minute-by-minute schedule of where to be and what to do. I was a grown adult being treated like a child; I was being told where to go and was walking there obediently. I had to turn off the TV when it got too late. I had to ask permission to use my belongings, and I had to come inside when the lights turned on. My choices and options were limited for my own good.

I had lived alone for decades. I feared the inability to ever be alone. In this facility, there were nurses and safety specialists present and attentive at all times. I saw my people every morning when I woke up and every night before bed. I never wanted to be alone again. It was safe, social, and communal.

I had come into the experience averaging six hours of low-quality sleep a night over a fourteen-year period. Each night on the unit, I was without phone, TV, or any other distraction in my room. I went to bed and woke up at the same time every night and had no alcohol in my system to mess with my sleep cycle. I got the best sleep of my life.

I began to love being there. I had never experienced anything like this before and felt so fortunate to be there. Five days in and five weeks ahead of my departure, I astutely predicted that going back into the real world would be very difficult.

The environment was safe. I was comfortable and content. All I had to do was "the hard work," as everyone called it.

Perhaps the best indication of how I felt is this picture I drew on day three. This masterpiece came into being during a class on mentalizing—which is a fancy word for thinking through someone's feelings, perspectives, emotions, and beliefs based on sensory cues that they provide. Try as they did to say that it wasn't, it's basically reading someone's mind. The assignment was for each patient to draw a picture that explained how they were feeling and then to present it without comment to the group and have them try to understand each peer's perspective.

Here's mine:

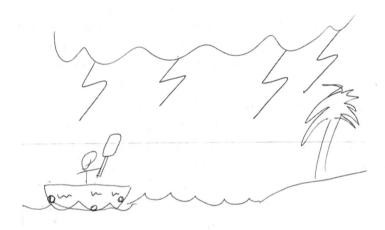

As you can see, I am a professional artist who takes his work very seriously. I understand that you'll probably want to rip out this page and frame it.

There were storms everywhere in my life that were not going away and were not escapable. I could weather the tempest, adrift in a raging sea in a leaky boat—or I could find footing on an island that provided at least some stability. In my mind, I was paddling to the island of the clinic to be as safe from as many threats as possible.

But either way, that storm was raging, and I couldn't last on the island forever.

It was time to find a steady ship and sail to safer weather.

CHAPTER II

THE FINER THINGS

Losing the small freedoms typically afforded to all non-incarcerated adults (free movement through doors and unsupervised sleep, to name a few) creates massive frustration. There were times when I'd internally scream when I was told, "No, you can't have dental floss in your room." That was a given. There was a benefit, however, in that the smallest things that I once took for granted became welcomed delights. By far, the two things that gave me the most daily joy were the meals and the workouts.

Our room and board covered three daily meals in the cafeteria, which served all five units on the campus. This was one of our few opportunities to get out of the unit and see "the others" (which included friends made at cross-unit courses, creative groups, and religious sessions). The cafeteria was a short walk away in the central building. Think of it as a corporate food hall with four hot stations, a salad bar, and one of those spinning dessert things like at the Golden Corral. I got made fun of considerably for only eating bagels, salads, and hummus every single day, but in a new place full of variables, I liked to control and simplify whatever I could (and not gain a bunch of weight, which proved surprisingly difficult even though I was forgoing five thousand-plus calories of alcohol per week).

I did become intermittently enamored with and heartbroken by a soft-serve ice cream machine. It was an unreliable apparatus that dispensed a bizarre duo of vanilla and pineapple flavors. It worked about 60 percent of the time, ran at its own speed, and sometimes quit mid-flow. But when that bad boy worked, man, did he hum. It took a few days, but I developed a dessert called the Prison McFlurry, which (as you can probably guess) is just a cup of soft serve with crumbles of cookie from the cabinet next to the drink machine. The ice cream was frozen vanilla medicine for my burning emotional tempest. I needed more. I lived on the edge to get it. The most daring act of defiance I attempted in my stay was smuggling soft serve out of the cafeteria in my water bottle. I was a criminal but not a smooth one. I was sniffed out immediately.

Breakfast was at 7:15 a.m. every day. Lunch was at 12:20 p.m. every day. Dinner was at 5:15 p.m. every day. We sat at the same tables every day. We walked to and from meals together in a pack, sometimes instinctively in a line like in grade school, each time escorted by staff members as per regulations. Those three-minute walks yielded some of the more meaningful conversations with my peers. It became common for me to inquire about the origin stories of new members of the cohort and why they joined us. Other times, we'd talk about our families and our careers, and how they fit into our mental health stories. There's nothing like the promise of a meal and an emergence into the great outdoors to get people to talk about what's really going on.

We were allowed some variety on the weekends when we pooled our money and ordered delivery for dinner. Think family favorites like pizza, Mexican, barbecue, and the occasional chain casual dining restaurant (P.F. Chang's was a go-to). The staff searched all the food that came in for contraband. All plastic bags and overly sharp items were confiscated, along with any loose drinks that a sneaky and benevolent delivery driver may have spiked with Tito's. I always looked forward to these meals. It felt like a party with friends—or at least it did compared to the rather drab cafeteria.

I legitimately miss meals together with my friends on the unit.

Much like trips to the cafeteria, our exercise time was also firmly structured, scheduled, and chaperoned. Each day included a one-hour scheduled trip to the gym and fifteen minutes of escorted walking time around the courtyard. Unfortunately, these fitness blocks were considered to be extremely soft by the schedulers, who had no problem popping a meeting with a doctor right on top of them. In an outstanding display of irony, I had to miss several gym sessions due to meetings with an eating and body image counselor. News flash: body image issues are not gender specific.

On the plus side, the gym facilities were well beyond expectations. Picture a high-end hotel workout room with numerous cardio machines, Nautilus equipment, and free weights. I became known for absolutely dominating the elliptical machine while locked into a thrashing Guns N' Roses playlist streaming through a very low-tech MP3 player issued by the facility. My friend Woody typically ellipticaled next to me. Little did he know I was competing with him for calorie-burn supremacy (it's always fun to win against somebody who doesn't know they're in a race with you).

After burning my legs to a crisp on the elliptical, I would venture through a glass door to a suspiciously high-quality basketball court (a donor must have been a baller). I had played basketball incessantly when I was young, but had been completely incompetent and embarrassingly yips-laden for the last two decades. I took this opportunity to practice and regain my skills, honed by self-challenges (I would count how many of the two hundred three-pointers I made) and epic HORSE showdowns with my peers Remy and Ace. Our (lack of) skills surely made the ghost of James Naismith vomit in disgust, but those games made us temporarily forget where we were and why. By the end of my time on campus, I had improved my basketball capability from "Sorry, man; this game is full" to "This dude is terrible but we need a player."

In those little moments, playing with my friends and eating together, it felt like we weren't patients but kids on the playground. The conversations, free from distraction from screens, made those times special and created connectivity not available in the real world. I really miss those times.

CHAPTER 12

DON'T FORGET ME WHEN I'M GONE

C heck the speech of any motivational speaker, life coach, or get-off-my-lawn old person, and it'll surely include some sentiment related to our reliance on technology, the lost art of in-person conversation and companionship, and the onslaught of information that we are presented with twenty-four hours a day. They challenge our kids to put their phones down and play outside, our adults to put differences aside and enjoy each other. These speeches are recorded via Zoom, hosted by partisan news networks, broadcast via YouTube, and watched on smartphones, and they feature a "click to subscribe" button so we can hear all their content as soon as it's available.

It's true that we are too connected. It's also true that we're never going to revert to the old way. It's swimming upstream; it's retrieving your carry-on out of the overhead when it's ten rows back from you. That's why communication restrictions made for an initially stressful and eventually glorious environment on the unit. One of my favorite party tricks is telling people I went six weeks without a phone, social media, or cable news and checking their reactions. It's equal parts horror, disbelief, and envy.

It was pretty simple—we could not have our personal mobile devices with us anywhere besides the nurses' station or approved privacy rooms.

Even then, there were very limited allotted times. Luckily, in one of the most bizarre parts of checking in, I received a burner flip phone. It was a bulky, black, screenless, modest connector to my friends and family that harkened back to 1997's best technology. These phones were far from smart. Let's call them intellectually challenged. No texting, no camera, and no internet, all for good reason (we were meant to focus on ourselves; plus, it helped maintain the confidentiality of our cohort). I used this prehistoric brick very sparingly. I must have called maybe ten different people in a total of thirty calls over six weeks. Some of my peers were more prolific in their flip phone utilization, particularly those with kids and spouses at home.

We did have access to our personal phones in the evenings during a limited number of thirty-minute, first-come-first-serve windows. I very rarely used mine, in deference to those who wanted to virtually tuck in their kids, talk to lawyers, or set up post-stay treatment. I checked my phone once a week, and every time it was a mistake. I would usually have about 100 unread notifications and 150 unread texts. Being drawn back into the real world for a fleeting moment was very difficult. It created sadness, FOMO, and regret, followed by the mini-shock of mentally reentering the unit and its restrictions. Plus, when better to disappear completely? I liked the idea of being unreachable.

Our primary form of communication was email, accessed on the public library-quality desktop computers. I tried to only check a couple of times a day, if at all. But as my little bro Jonathan and I later discussed, email is really a great lost form of communication. It provides the convenience, control, and craftsmanship of asynchronous communication and contains much more information than texts and DMs. Maybe it's time to bring back the personal email.

The '90s technology lifestyle vibes extended beyond the communications. In a fantastic retreat from the hideous epidemic of too much information, we never, ever watched cable news. If something was important enough to need to know it, we'd know it. We had some local and national newspapers delivered daily, and we checked news websites every now and then. We occasionally glimpsed social media on someone's personal phone, but only to see a picture of a kid or a car. We spent time getting to know each other face to face in our downtime and found time. We knew more about each other than adults typically would ever learn—stuff that was deep below the surface and not about work. It was wonderful.

A lot of us '80s kids lament that the modern youth doesn't live like we did. We shake our proverbial fists from our imaginary rocking chairs on our imaginary front porches, complaining that modern kids don't ride bikes until the lights come on. We tell tales of riding six hours in a station wagon with no entertainment but the alphabet game, sitting at boring dinners with only a crayon and a paper place mat to hold our attention, and reveling in the five television channels we received over an antenna. And yet, with all the screens in the world, kids say they're bored.

We are a unique generation in that when we were teenagers, all of the information in the world—positive, destructive, true, and false—became available to us. I can confirm that anxiety-inducing media-generated and user-generated content has not been good for me. The addition of constant comparison, debate, and FOMO into the psychological mixing bowl between my ears is a bad recipe. I have to think it's the same for others. The number-one learning and reflection I've shared with people about my experience is how cleansing it was to go from a stimulus firehose to a trickle.

I'd be just fine with the neighborhood grapevine, which was pretty effective. Our generation managed to spread misinformation about Mikey from the Life cereal commercial and Richard Gere without the aid of social media.

CHAPTER 13

WHAT'S ON YOUR MIND

When I was in high school, we had an assembly featuring a dude who was some sort of ambassador or businessman or person with some other reason for knowing a lot about China. As with any forced learning event, there was a robust question-and-answer session at the conclusion of the prepared remarks. Being that this was a rather stuffy private school with a bougie reputation to uphold, the faculty carefully handpicked a set of questions and presentable scholars to recite them.

Amid the drab, stab-me-in-the-eyes-please queries about economic development, cultural evolution, and government philosophies came the voice of an angel of spontaneity to break the agony. She was not among the prescreened set, instead grabbing attention with a traditional hand raise. With a sturdy and confident voice from the back of the auditorium came her amazing inquiry: "So, like, are there squirrels in China?"

The inquisitor was a well-known free spirit and something of a mascot of her class. She took some grief from teachers for being a silly heart and from jealous peers who accused her of being a shameless attention-seeker. I, for one, considered her a treasure on our campus and in that assembly. The question was received with a mix of groans from the haters and laughs and cheers from her supporters (including me).

Free speech and academic curiosity were squashed that day as a frazzled teacher quickly called on another student (who probably asked about cross-continental economic development or something). I was left a bit stunned as I never heard an answer. Are there squirrels in China? Why wouldn't they allow an answer? Was the question deemed so dumb that everyone must already know the answer? But given that nobody in the audience actually knew the answer, was there a risk that the speaker didn't know either? Was there a nefarious rodent-based conspiracy at risk of being uncovered? Who was being protected?

This moment taught me a critical principle in life: don't be afraid to ask the question that others aren't asking for fear of looking uninformed or plain dumb. Most of the time, others in the room don't know the answer either; they want to know the answer and would be better off for knowing it. Having sat in many boardrooms full of people grappling to be the smartest in the room, I find that these questions are typically never asked. Instead, there are complex and "smart-sounding" questions that are really proclamations of "look how smart I am for even asking this brilliant inquiry."

I just looked it up. It turns out there *are* squirrels in China, including the Chinese giant flying squirrel (*Petaurista xanthotis*), among many others.

The point of all this is that I'm going to answer some questions I have received about my time in the psych ward. A lazy device for presenting a lot of information in an efficient way? Yep. It's also efficient, sortable, and skimmable if you don't need to know the answer to a specific question.

Did Anybody Try to Escape?

Short answer: Yes, successfully (at least for a while).

The facility that I went to was a voluntary one, which meant that anyone could leave whenever they wanted with forty-eight-hour advance notice. However, that did not stop two people in different units from scaling the twelve-foot wall surrounding the back patio. We still don't know quite how it happened, and of course we got nothing out of the nurses or security staff (the only way we knew was from overheard radio chatter and hushed conversations at the nurses' station). It was remarkable how the half-complete information spread prolifically, like in elementary school when you heard that Cody's dad was in the Mafia and their family was in witness protection and that was why they moved from New Jersey to Charlotte and Cody had some of his dad's guns and he had a girlfriend at another school and they French kissed.

There was no risk of escape among the tenants of my unit. We were not nearly motivated or athletic enough. But that didn't mean we weren't subjected to lockdowns when breakout attempts occurred elsewhere on campus or if a new patient joined our group and was at risk. This happened a couple of times, including when my close friend Ace joined. On Ace's first evening, I became vocally frustrated that I couldn't go onto the back porch and couldn't get an answer from the staff as to why not. I was an annoying little kid who wanted to know everything and wouldn't listen to "because I said so" from the nurse. I didn't know that we were contained indoors when there were new patients with suicide risk. As it was his first day and he didn't know me, Ace pegged me for a hothead who would be tough to deal with. In the end, he was glad to find out I was ignorant and not chronically angry.

To follow up, one of the escapees was found at a nearby gas station and the other went to their parents' house. Given the rather rough neighborhood where the facility was located, these were probably the best-case scenarios.

Were There Any Romances?

Short answer: Absolutely not, but the unit rules made it clear that it had happened before.

I applaud anyone who is in the mindset to run a game while in a psych ward, but for all of us in the unit at the time, it was completely unimaginable. Starting with the demographic reality—most of us were male. Many were married; some were recently divorced. Even having to explain this feels pretty gross because we felt like family. I can say with certainty there was nothing close to resembling romance in our unit.

That doesn't mean it didn't happen elsewhere on campus, particularly in the units with Gen Z patients. Nothing says "healthy dating environment" like hormone-crazed teens and twenty-somethings, each with a psychological disorder serious enough to land them in a secure institution.

However, we *were* subjected to some interesting rules that conjured ideas about previous history. We were never allowed, under any circumstance, to go into another patient's room. We couldn't take blankets into common rooms, let alone share one with a peer. And if it wasn't clear enough that you couldn't bunk up or get handsy in public with one of your temporary roommates, there was an outright rule about not canoodling. One time, Pablo and I speculated about whether it would be at all possible to complete a physical rendezvous even if you desperately wanted to. Between the house rules, the every-fifteen-minutes vigilance, and the complete lack of privacy, we concluded it was impossible; people would have to be shamelessly bold to try.

But again, those rules existed for a reason. If those walls could talk, I would 1) check my meds for hallucination tendencies and 2) tell them to shut up because I really didn't want to know what had happened on the brown fabric couch.

Could You Have Visitors?

Short answer: Yes, but not like in the movies.

When I imagined visitors during my stay, I pictured something like the scene in *The Fugitive* when Dr. Richard Kimble speaks to inmate Clive Driscoll through the glass at the jail, or *Brokedown Palace* when Claire Danes's friends (a group that included Paul Walker) yell across a chasm through chicken wire. In reality, there was a comfortable room with some couches just inside the unit door, where friends and family could spend an hour with their committed loved ones. A few couches, a TV, a table for outside food, etc.

Patients who were local to the area had a number of visitors, and everyone had at least someone travel in to visit. I only had one session of visitors, as I did not really want anyone going out of their way for such a short visit, nor did I really want anyone to see me in these circumstances. Two of my friends local to that city brought me a poke bowl, some car magazines, and sixty minutes of conversation about the real world. It was a nice distraction, but I never wanted another visitor. The process made it feel more like an incarceration than a hospital stay.

What Did You Miss the Most about Home?

Short answer: Events with friends and family, whether big or small.

I walked into the doors of the clinic on the Wednesday before Easter, so I was faced with the worst part of the experience early. Easter has always been a time of gathering, celebrating, and pastels. The rest of my crowd was in Atlanta at Elizabeth's house monitoring an egg hunt among the cousins, preparing a festive feast, and enjoying a beautiful spring day outdoors. I was in a drab, tiny chapel with a motley crew of strangers, and the best part of my day was a short walk to the cafeteria. With that said, the nurses did hide Easter eggs for us, which I thought was really sweet.

I missed the little moments. Walks on Bayshore Boulevard, gathering my friends by my pool, date nights. This feeling waned as the weeks passed and I grew my relationships with my cohort. I came to appreciate the daily and weekly moments and rituals that I was uniquely experiencing, almost to the point where I felt like my circle on the outside should have FOMO.

Could You Order Stuff Online?

Short answer: Yes, and the snacks and junk food were dangerous.

Red in *The Shawshank Redemption* would be out of work inside this particular facility. As long as you kept your identity hidden (first name, last name, unit, patient number) in your address and understood your deliveries were subject to search and confiscation, you could buy whatever you wanted online. The same screening policy was in place for packages and letters from home. I made sure that my mom did not send me a pound cake full of belts and shoelaces—that would have been really embarrassing.

Over the course of my stay, I ordered a mattress cover, pillows, nail clippers (immediately stored in the secure closet), an electric razor (samesies), granola bars, and a full boatload of snacks. Everyone ordered snacks. The unit was crammed with junk food. Combine that with the aforementioned lethargy of life on the unit, and perhaps it was a good thing that we didn't have belts.

Were There Any Famous/Infamous People in There?

Short answer: Nobody in my cohort was famous or infamous, but that didn't mean they weren't interesting.

We heard fables from the staff of nameless, unidentifiable celebrities and high-profile people. One particularly humorous story was about a patient who wouldn't reveal their real name, even when their face would appear on TV while the group was watching the news. They never acknowledged that their face was on the screen.

I absolutely was pulling for a celeb before starting the program. Knowing what I know now, I loved that we were all anonymous, unknown to each other, and able to get to know each other more deeply with no preconceived biases. We had high-profile people within narrow communities, which made for just as fascinating tales as any movie star would have. We just didn't have the paparazzi flying helicopters over the quad.

Update: It turns out that one member of my cohort was portrayed in a very popular Netflix series. It was a dramatized account of the life of an extremely infamous American, in which my friend Ward played a heroic role. The actor looked nothing like him.

Did You Feel Ashamed to Be There?

Short answer: Yes, in the first few days, but absolutely not in the long run.

Most of my tears and exasperation about my descent into such an extreme measure were expunged during the forty-eight hours after checking in. In that period, during any quiet moment, there was a risk of panic. I had the sense of denial that I was there. I looked at my cohort and felt out of place. I even felt a bit of fear or intimidation about who I was dealing with, since I didn't know anyone's story or condition.

It didn't take long to understand that everyone felt the same way as I did, and all we wanted to do was support each other and normalize our experiences. We used a number of coping mechanisms to expel the shame from our group and anyone who joined it. We would speak to new admits about how we felt in their shoes. We reassured each other that we were in a safe place, in a safe group, and completely without judgment. We reminded each other that so many could benefit from taking a similar step but either were not strong enough or didn't have the resources. We considered ourselves fortunate.

Above all, we laughed. The situations we faced were so ridiculous that all we could do was laugh. We joked about scaring new patients by acting loopy and spewing gibberish. I decided I would stand in front of the aerial images on the television screen savers and invite a new admit to come fly with me. We mentally designed alumni merchandise, bumper stickers that said, "I'm Crazy for the Mental Hospital!" We ribbed each other, watched funny movies, and experienced everyday silliness like anyone would in or out of a psych ward. Like Jimmy Buffett said, if we couldn't laugh, we would all go insane. We were already considered insane, so we may as well laugh.

What Was the Music Situation Given How Important It Is to You?

The banning of our personal communication devices naturally meant that we did not have access to our digital library of audio and visual stimulation. This had the potential to be extremely problematic for me, given the role of music in my life as motivator, soother, and concentration wrangler. I couldn't get a straight answer ahead of time on how I would solve the issue, which obviously created substantial anxiety. Fortunately, along with our flip phones, we were also issued streaming music devices designed for small children. Hence, they had no web browsing, camera, or communication capabilities.

They got the job done. My little blue player, numbered 01, was pre-loaded with Spotify. All seemed well as I was able to listen to Guns N' Roses while working out, Chromatics while being pensive, and Bill Simmons podcasts to feel normal and "at home." I did become frustrated by the commercials, as I was initially unable to log out of the previous user's account. This wasn't a huge deal until I looked up a podcast and noticed this person's search history. Let's just say that there's a whole universe of podcasts that appeal to, shall we say, "lonely and physically needy" listeners. I gave the device a good cleaning, both physically and digitally, and was eventually able to log in for myself.

I consider it a unique privilege to be able to answer all of my friends' and family's questions regarding what it's like in a psych ward. I revel in the variety of inquiries and the ingoing expectations of the answers—most of which are contrary to the ultimate truth, which was that my experience was, on balance, a very positive one. I find myself smiling and becoming energized when I hear curiosity because it gives me an opportunity to share my memories. Sometimes people will lead with "You don't have to answer this, but . . ." I have never denied an unfiltered response. By the time the question-and-answer sessions are complete, it's not unusual to hear the interrogator conclude that it's something that they or someone close to them should consider. I'm always eager to follow up and tell more stories.

CHAPTER 14

TOUCH OF GRAY

After the initial rush of newness, fear, uncertainty, anxiety, and caf-eteria food wears off, there was nothing but time and therapy on the unit. The idea of five and a half weeks inside a single compound was daunting in the early days.

During the second half of the stay, the repetition and sameness begins to take a toll. I began to resent the feeling of being trapped, the lack of movement, the footstool on my movie-watching chair that moved around too much—small nuisances grew into monumental pains with no new stimuli available.

Without realizing it, I had become part of the scenery. As new people came through, I became an old soul, a sage longtimer. As evenings came, my friends naturally looked to me for guidance on what we would watch. Inside jokes and unspoken etiquette became part of the culture. I moved through the days and nights with the comfort and ease of a person whose lifetime was spent in a single environment—one who worried about adjusting to another change in environment. In my case, I feared a return to my old life.

Journal entry: Sunday, May 8, 2022

Tired. Tired. Tired

By every definition

Bored. Trapped. Still safe. Still happy

But so, so bored. Making me exhausted

There was literally nothing to do Saturday, only a few Sunday

Starting to pull away. The group is changing

Like being a senior in high school

People you look up to leave

Replaced with people you don't know, don't get to know

But I'm still glad to be here

I was the newest patient on the unit for about a week. For a full seven days, I felt like a pledge, a freshman, a rookie. I revered the two women who were about to leave as sage, regally aloof leaders who seemed above it all. Not in a snobbish way, but in the way of an experienced and elevated achiever who has seen it all. I was shocked how, in only five weeks, they attained such status. Don't get me wrong; they were wonderful, gracious, and approachable people. They simply didn't have the emotional energy to invest too much into me. I never thought I'd be that way.

As the newness wanes, repetition and boredom wax. Once I had seen the cycle and cadence of a few weeks, it became physically exhausting at times. And as new citizens immigrated into our small nation, I naturally became less invested in their incorporation and adjustment. I cared for them, and I became close with a few of them, but I left the day-to-day mentorship to the newer patients.

Senioritis had not fully set in by this point, but I finally understood the mindset of those upperclassmen and the women I met on the first day.

Journal entry: Wednesday, May 11, 2022

The days run together

Minutes crawl, hours tick, days fly

The mood is light

Things feel good

The light is out there

Home awaits

I'm the president of the unit now

I wake up feeling so safe here

It's a happy place. It can be

I'm so thankful when I wake up here

"Vibe" is an overused word in that it's uttered more than zero times a day. I will make one exception here—the vibe on the unit changed day to day and week to week. There are a number of factors that impacted the mood:

- Whether there was a group therapy session that day (two days per week) and if there was a conflict therein, healthy or unhealthy.
- The connectivity and compatibility of the overall group, the composition of which changed every few days with an entry or an exit.
- The moods of individual people, particularly those who tended to lead the culture (I was one of them, and two others also played a large part).
- If it was a Saturday or a Sunday, which were the most unstructured and unpredictable days. It was a balance of the low of boredom and the high of delivered food.
- The weather, which determined time spent in the sun or total containment under the fluorescent lights.
- Which staff members were working (there were fun ones and not-so-fun ones).

Mercury's status in the planetary order was not a factor.

It's worth noting that on this day of the journal entry (May 11), I rose to the hallowed, prestigious status of President of the Unit for the week. I would love to tell you that there was a hard-fought election and a speech. In reality, the title simply goes in order of seniority, and it was my turn. The president is the emcee of our twice-a-day check-in meetings and our once-a-week community meeting with the staff. I did my best to set an orderly and fun tone. I even had a platform that included a decree that meetings start on time regardless of attendance and that a committee would be created to determine a new activity for the upcoming Saturday. Promises made and promises kept—both regarding timeliness and activity (we created a mission to check off viewing the American Film Institute's Top 100 Movies of All Time).

Journal entry: Friday, May 13, 2022

It feels really nice here. Comfortable

Except my Achilles which hurts terribly

These are good people

I will miss this. Treasure it

I won't even have pictures

There's nothing like this. Nothing

About a week before leaving, it became clear that I was going to miss being there. Fridays were always good days. Even though we weren't working per se, there was a feeling of quittin' time for the weekend after finishing the last of our weekly therapies. While it's not on the record, I have to believe that day involved some good belly laughs, some emotional or actual hugs, and some good breakthroughs shared. And if my Achilles was hurting that badly, it meant I had played some serious basketball.

It hit me that in 2022, in a world where we have images and videos of every five-year-old tee ball game from multiple angles, I would not have any photos of my time there. The only way to memorialize what I knew would become such a permanent fixture in my life was to etch it through writing. During the last week of my stay and up until right now, I have done my best to record everything that I remember in as vivid detail as possible. As the weeks pass, things that I forgot come popping back into my mind. I don't love it. It happens in weird ways. Yesterday I saw a broken ceramic flowerpot and remembered that there were no ceramic flowerpots (you can break them and create sharp objects). I have a feeling I'll experience flashbacks like that one for a long time.

Over those weeks, I learned firsthand how no matter where you are or what situation you are in, a cultural and social construct will develop. I was a mainstay of ours. I had social status. I had clear roles, and I had value I couldn't offer to the same degree anywhere else. I became an old soul, a fixture, and a prominent member of our population. It didn't matter that it was a psych ward. I was somebody important. It's hard to leave that behind without some sadness and longing, both of which grew each day as my release date approached.

CHAPTER 15

THAT'S WHAT FRIENDS ARE FOR

Journal entry: Tuesday, May 10, 2022

So much laughter today from start to finish

It was just so great. Felt like a group of friends

Inside jokes, good times

This is what I will look back on

Appreciate the moments

Crosswords in the day room, walks to meals

These are good times

By the third week inside, it became hard to distinguish the days. I was told before going in that it becomes Groundhog Day, which was true. Instead of Ned Ryerson pestering me about insurance, it was a nurse with a blood pressure cuff, and instead of "I've Got You Babe," it was chronically deafening silence. Sometimes it felt like a week had passed in a two-hour span; sometimes you blinked and it was the weekend.

Weekends meant something, even in a pretend world where nobody worked (except for the medical staff; they definitely worked). While each weekday was booked solidly from 8:30 a.m. until 8:30 p.m., the weekends only contained chunks of planned activities suspended in an unstructured Jell-O mold. For a group of people who were permanent residents in their own heads and missing out on lives in the real world, the frequent sedentary boredom proved very challenging.

I enjoyed weekends. Two of my favorite scheduled events occurred on the weekends. Every Saturday we had a music therapy class, which spoke to me far more than most of the cognitive challenges and techniques. There were different exercises each session, which always involved connecting emotions with music and lyrics. One Saturday, we each came prepared with a song that was deeply meaningful to us and had the group speculate on the feelings and emotions that each song conjured. Then, we explained the reality of what each song meant to us. Pablo chose a verbally aggressive yet surprisingly touching Eminem song. My friend Cecelia chose a hymn I can't remember. I chose "Brandy (You're a Fine Girl)" by Looking Glass because it's exceptional yacht rock, and it reminded me of wonderful times that I miss at the lake. I also really wanted to hear it on a loudspeaker that day. It was another Shawshank-inmates-on-the-roof moment when it felt like a group of friends enjoying real life, if only for a moment.

Ask almost anyone on·the unit and they'd tell you that our Sunday afternoon bocce ball was a high point of the week. We'd go out to the side yard and assemble a bootleg court using yoga mats, beanbags, and sticks. Even the most withdrawn and struggling members of our group turned up for these bocce showdowns. My friend Ward was almost always physically and emotionally drained, sometimes incapable of emerging from his room for days at a time. But on the bocce ball court, he was LeBron James willing his team to victory. For one hour, we felt like a group of friends in a park, laughing and playfully junk talking, only without the beer and grilling normally present. The staff would often join us, making it extra fun and giving us an opportunity to get to know them better. As one of them quipped, "The only difference between y'all and us is that we have keys."

Aside from these scheduled events, weekends involved a lot of series binging, tracking sports we didn't particularly care about on TV, reading, puzzles, and doing anything we could to pass the time. One weekend, we weeded the garden on the back patio. I did all of the above plus a lot of writing and planning for my time back home. Above all, I took the opportunity to let my brain take a rest from the psychological archaeology and calisthenics of the week.

We spent a lot of downtime together watching television. There were three places to watch TV on the unit—the large, high-ceilinged common room and each of the breakout rooms on either side. The televisions featured every conceivable streaming service, plus a respectable cable lineup, so there was no shortage of options. The real challenge was finding programming that was agreeable, noncontroversial, and balanced to the demands of our diverse group.

The common room TV was almost exclusively tuned to sports or *The Office* for two main reasons. First, by process of elimination—we never watched cable news so as not to create any arguments; we couldn't have any overtly violent or sexual content airing, and I assume most of you have watched TV lately; and it was hard to stream anything with a complex plot or dense information with people coming and going. Second, I was one of the only people who knew how to operate the remotes. Hence, we watched a lot of sports and *The Office*.

One of the TV-appointed breakout rooms was used primarily for private conversations, meditation, or phone calls, so we were left with only one other room for entertainment. Each afternoon, we discussed a viewing plan. Usually, a group of five or six of us would binge a popular limited series or choose a new blockbuster or beloved classic movie to take in. We popped popcorn, ate snacks, and laughed. We laughed a lot. Some of my best memories are from these moments with my friends.

Pablo and I were usually the last to go to bed. It felt like an elementary school sleepover—two kids trying to stay awake as late as we could (or at least until the midnight TV-off rule) just because we could. Between episodes, we learned about each other, talked about our lives at home, or just acted like a couple of immature middle-aged dudes.

Our routine and our home became more comfortable with time. Over the weeks, I explored our space and, dare I say, pushed boundaries on what was possible to feel a little freer. Patients earned more rights as we proved our stability and responsibility. For their first twenty-four hours, everyone started locked in the unit. After two weeks, we could earn the right to walk the grounds in groups with other experienced patients. The height of liberty was solo outdoor excursions as long as we rang the doorbell every fifteen minutes, kind of like when Paul Newman was shaking the tree in *Cool Hand Luke*. We weren't exactly explorers—we could only walk on the sidewalks connecting the units and the quarter-mile walking track surrounding the courtyard. The fruits of our work and diligence amounted to the ability to traverse to the vending machine on campus.

As my cohort became able, we spent more time outside, whether on walks or just to sit in the sun for fresh air and breeze. The unit had a front porch with a view of the sunset as the sun dipped below the outer wall of the facility. Once we earned the right, Ace, Floyd, and I would relax on plastic outdoor chairs after a hard day of introspection. We'd tell stories about our lives at home. We'd laugh about the absurdity of things we had experienced inside, like the one nighttime patient safety associate who, during his fifteen-minute safety checks, would linger near the TV any time the movie scene got racy. It was not subtle. We felt like a group of friends, maybe neighbors enjoying a cold one on a Friday evening (without the cold one). It was another small moment that made us feel normal.

There were also some extremely poignant and difficult moments that we shared with each other. While we were shielded from reality in our dome, real-life problems were still out in the world and seeping through our walls. Several friends had ongoing marital issues. One friend had a very serious pending legal issue. We would do the best we could to support each other with the limited amount of data that we had about each other.

The toughest support moment I had was when Ward sat down at the lunch table and quietly announced to the group that his wife was leaving him. He and I had grown close in spite of a significant gap in age and life experiences. I abandoned my tray, walked over to him, and put my hand on his shoulder. I invited him to go on a walk with me. He was struggling physically. We slowly walked and talked, just the two of us, and tried to make sense of what was happening. We sat on the front porch of the unit. He quietly wept; I told him what a good man he was. As the rest of the group came back from lunch, each offered a hand, a hug, an encouraging word. I wept for him. It was the first time in years I felt that much emotion toward another person's pain. My hard shell was breaking away.

As I neared the end of my time inside the psych ward, I already started missing these moments. I became close friends with a group of strangers who helped me through the hardest stretch of my life. I can't help but wonder how different the years leading up to my admission to the unit could have been if I were as honest with myself and others on the outside as I was with my cohort inside.

It's not productive to think about that alternate universe. That is not how the story went.

IV.

Brilliant Disguise

CHAPTER 16

I STILL HAVEN'T FOUND
WHAT I'M LOOKING FOR

Nobody told me how important dress socks are to mobility and sur-
vival. I received countless warnings about wardrobe requirements
and errors when moving to a place with subfreezing temperatures. I purchased enough North Face gear to outfit an entire fraternity pledge class.
I had face coverings before they were required and ubiquitous. Every
time I walked the half mile from my apartment to campus, I felt like
the little brother in *A Christmas Story*, bundled to the point of losing
range of motion. I even knew the trick about having one giant coat over
a T-shirt so as not to burn to death once inside the fiery, heated confines
of the classroom.

My blind spot was dress socks. When you attend a master of business administration program, particularly one of some level of repute,
you should know you need to have a formal ensemble fit for the local
climate. Interview season was generally in January and February at
Northwestern University's MBA program (or simply "Kellogg" when
trying to name drop), and many of these interviews occurred off-cam-
pus, requiring a walk/cross-country ski in the wild. I learned the importance of warm foot coverings for business formal attire the hard way as
I walked to an 8:30 a.m. interview at the Hotel Orrington. It was a mere

quarter mile away from base camp, but even a few minutes of exposure in the zero-degree air would create real problems.

Wearing only the thin dress socks I had last worn during summer weddings in Charleston and Savannah, my nervous, ball-of-energy-self trekked down the recently de-iced sidewalk to face my fate at my dream employer. When I say dream employer, let's be clear that I didn't grow up drawing pictures of myself as a management consultant in business casual and a vest, leading workshops in front of glazed-over clients. But in MBA parlance, this employer was Stark Industries to all the insecure overachievers (including me).

Sure enough, halfway to my destination, my toes went numb. Walking became difficult. My footing—already unsteady from my inner Stilwell from *A League of Their Own* telling me, "You're gonna loooooose. Yooouuu stiiiiiink"—became that much more unsteady. I vowed to never again underestimate the need to protect fingers and toes, if only I could make it to my destination without taking a tumble. God was looking out for me as I arrived on my useless feet, but the HVAC deities at the hotel decided to prolong the adventure by impairing the heating system. A thermostat in the interview holding tank displayed forty-one degrees. There was no escape from the cold.

Any tactile discomfort I endured from subfreezing temperatures was my own fault. I readily and enthusiastically chose to move to Chicago over warmer locales in North Carolina and Virginia. My MBA school application process ran parallel to my father's illness in the fall and spring of 2005 and 2006. I was not satisfied with my standing in the professional world, and I believed I needed a jump start to accelerate my career. Said another way, I wanted to buy a prestige stamp and a chance to upgrade my job, presumably to a more glamorous financial institution than the one where I was employed. I applied to a wide range of schools, some realistic and some overly ambitious. I got into three and a half schools (waitlisted at one; I'll get back at you one day, Michigan).

Choosing an MBA program from multiple options is generally pretty simple—you go to the best one you get into. Yeah, I get it—there are scholarships, industry-specific areas of focus, geographic needs, and irrational decision-making processes. But y'all need to chill. I'm just generalizing here, and you know I'm not wrong. Up to that point in my life, I would've chosen to stay closer to home given my risk-averse nature and guardrails. But with my father no longer as a limiter, I became the simple guy who went to the best one I got into. It just happened to be located squarely in the North Pole.

A prestigious MBA program is pretty easy to explain. It's also equally perplexing as to how it's a real thing that is widely accepted as a productive activity by which parents and peers are impressed. It's a completely voluntary and profoundly expensive two-year alternate universe. Hundreds of men and women in their late twenties return to a college life where grades don't matter, in classes that many have either already taken or don't find particularly difficult. Most students abandon lucrative positions to instead go into six-figure debt yet spend as if they are still gainfully employed. The costs of theme parties and spring break trips around the globe are considered an "investment" in networking and experiences. Bar tabs run high, sleep runs late, and reality seems distant.

Against all odds, these same irrational adults are sought out by the most prestigious investment banks, management consultancies, and blue-chip corporations around the world. These institutions send large teams to campus to lure new recruits with logo merchandise and free food, raining USB drives and Panera sandwiches to impress the best and brightest.

In keeping with my original "be/outdo my dad" plan, I conducted perfunctory, cursory, and painful networking attempts with the Wall Street investment banks. It felt empty, pointless, and unproductive. I finally admitted to myself that I had no interest in that job or career path. It was a taste of the freedom that was a byproduct of my father's death—I could finally chart my own course and pursue a career that I believed would fit my needs. And, to be clear, my needs were to receive massive outward validation and to prove that I was successful. Only now I was free to do so in a job that I wouldn't have had to explain. Cue the siren song of management consulting.

The on-campus corporate mating ritual is most aggressively practiced by the representatives of the management consulting industry. I
knew relatively nothing about this industry when I started my MBA program. Once I learned more, I believed it was a perfect match for somebody who had no idea what he wanted to do with his career, wanted to
learn an endless amount of content and management skills, and loved
Patagonia vests. As if the industry was designed for people like me who
had a bottomless need for validation, these managing consulting recruit-
ers promised constant evaluation and opportunities for promotions to
spectacular titles like "Engagement Manager" and "Associate Director."
Without the specter of my dad hovering over me, I quickly became one
of the converted masses huddling at the altar of management consulting.

Here's how to best summarize management consulting:

- Multi-multi-multi-billion-dollar professional services machine.
- Led by three elite firms that spend copious amounts of money to
  attract and recruit the best, the brightest, and me.
- Paid silly fees by Fortune 500 companies to develop strategies
  that the companies take credit for when they work and the management consultants bear the blame for when they don't.

And here's how to best summarize their target employees:

- Insecure overachievers.
- Graduates of fancy schools (without the self-punishment gene
  required for banking or the risk-tolerance gene required for
  startups).
- Excited by prestige, airline status, and logoed messenger bags.

I threw myself into the maelstrom of the recruiting process. There
were about a dozen of these organizations but there were three for which
most MBAs strived. In typical insecure Michael fashion, I assumed I
would not be considered worthy of those three, so I took the shotgun
approach. For two months, almost every day was filled with information

sessions, "coffee chats" (brutally uncomfortable one-on-one sessions between distracted junior consultants and overly eager, suited recruits), and cheesy networking events. With all the branded merchandise bestowed upon us, no rain would touch my head, and no key of mine would be unchained. And I would never need a pen again.

All the interactions included references to the mysterious, pressure-filled, and critically important case interviews. Hushed tones, reverence, and intimidation swirled around these forty-five-minute interrogations meant to replicate the skillset of the management consultant. The interviewer presents the subject with a "real" business situation. The interviewee must extract information and make a reasonable recommendation for how to resolve it. Candidates must learn a specific and unspoken language, sequence, and etiquette associated with this evaluative dance. This is usually accomplished by doing scores of mock interviews with peers who also have no idea what they are doing. Occasionally, you get to practice with an actual living, breathing, sage consultant who was in the exact same boat less than a year prior. Needless to say, the whole rigmarole is preposterous.

In the end, I interviewed with only those three prestigious firms. In the frothy pre-meltdown economy of 2007, they would have interviewed just about any warm body. From there, I received invitations from two of them to do a final follow-up round of interviews (the third one cut me *during* my first-round interview). I suppose my preparation for the case interview and my raw eagerness paid off.

One day after receiving the news that I would have follow-ups at both, I interviewed for the clear-cut most prestigious firm (at the time), which also happened to be the only one with an office in Charlotte. In spite of my crippling self-doubt and the nagging Stilwell in my ear, I managed to secure an offer for the summer internship. I remember receiving the phone call in my apartment and dropping to my knees in relief, disbelief, and gratitude that I had not, in fact, thrown my career and $150,000 away to attend business school.

Three days later, I was nervously interviewing at the other firm. Objectively, the pressure was off with the competitor's offer in hand.

But this was the firm I had long dreamed of working for. I was drawn to the culture, the people, and the firm's stance as a fighter against the number-one firm. I found the people in the Dallas office, which I was targeting, to be *my* people (and I believe vice versa based on the fact that they were already calling me "Stutts"). One senior partner in particular became a fast mentor and friend, and not just because he was also a Tar Heel and from Shelby, North Carolina (you'll remember that's where I spent my weekends with my grandparents). He genuinely felt like a big brother, like family. He would become one of the most important influences in my life.

The aforementioned freezing-cold, toe-numbing walk to the igloo of a hotel conference room was the lead-up to my big interview, my chance, my One Shining Moment. Over the next three hours, I chattered, shivered, and babbled my way through those dreaded case interviews. To mental fireworks and fanfare, a few days later, I received a phone call with an offer for an internship at what would become my employer for ten years and a summer.

The decision to go to Dallas versus Charlotte was excruciating. On paper, it was a no-brainer. Why wouldn't I be going to the "best" firm that had an office in my hometown, the city where I always intended to live? Why would I go to a city where I knew nobody (Dallas), and say no to an offer from a firm that literally none of the previous year's offerees had declined (fact)? I badly wanted to go to Dallas with the people I already considered friends, and the logical voice of my father pleaded with me to take the Charlotte offer. But that was not a real voice anymore. In a bold act of defiance against absolutely no living person, I took the Dallas offer, and off I went.

That summer, thirty or so Dallas office interns and I made our first steps toward becoming a partner and managing director at the firm. Of those thirty, three would eventually make it. I wasn't thinking that far ahead, as I still felt like my offer was an administrative error. Most of my classmates were from schools that Jessie Spano wanted to attend. They were polished, serious, and driven. Like Milton with his red stapler, I was sure they'd "fix the glitch" posthaste. I channeled the sixteen-year-old kid at City Chevrolet, vowing to work harder than anyone else to prove my value and that I belonged.

As an intern, one is expected to do whatever is asked, no matter how ridiculous, to generate insights and data for our clients. I had the single most preposterous task I ever saw in my ten years in that job.

I had spent the summer visiting jewelry stores around the country to benchmark the experience, even going so far as to pretend to buy an engagement ring for a fellow intern (in real life, it was even weirder than it sounds). Interesting as it might have been, it didn't offer an opportunity to show off analytical acuity. I spent the first eight of the ten weeks on unsure footing without a meaningful and challenging "at-bat" to show what I could do. My moment came on August 13, 2007, when a high-stakes meeting with our client was moved forward by a week, therefore requiring a full-team all-nighter to prepare a very large PowerPoint deck that nobody would read. My retail sleuthing put me in the perfect position to write one slide describing, in fine detail, the points of brand differentiation within our client's portfolio. My project manager gave me the assignment at around midnight, and like Frank the Tank in the *Old School* debate scene, I blacked out while I wrote brilliant, insightful, and pithy brand manifestos. At 2:15 a.m., I heard a holler from the next room over: "Stutts, this is, like, perfect. You nailed it. Great work. No edits." I had made it.

I did not expect that a single slide and a few people I worked with would set the course for the remainder of my management consulting tenure (and in many ways, the rest of my career). My consumer-focused mindset led to my appointment to more than fifty engagements in the retail, restaurant, and travel sectors. My work ethic earned me the right to take on more responsibility earlier than others. The senior partner who recruited me became one of the five or so most senior leaders in the entire firm. The project manager who praised the single slide became one of the most globally influential partners in my areas of focus. A few lucky breaks, along with some extremely hard work beyond anything of which I thought I was capable, led to a fast rise in title, income, and status.

Over the next several years, I graduated through the ranks and experienced some pretty wild stuff. The founder of a very prominent quick service restaurant chain let me drive his three-million-dollar Ferrari LaFerrari. I sat at the helm of the largest cruise ship in the world. I ate Wonder Bread right off the factory line. I wrote a script used at thousands of hotel check-in desks around the world (I heard it used while checking into a Paris hotel once; that was cool). I conducted consumer interviews on Laguna Beach. I sat in a windowless conference room while listening to the FBI raid a client's office and take all the computers. I could go on for pages. Needless to say, I had some unique and inexplicably weird experiences.

Most people associate consulting with crazy amounts of travel, and that's correct. But please, please do not think that *Up in the Air* is an accurate representation. There is simply no way that the George Clooney character would fly ten million miles going between Peoria, Des Moines, and Chicago. In total, I experienced roughly 1,600 takeoffs and landings and spent about 1,200 nights in hotel rooms. I attended internal and client meetings in fifteen countries. Sadly, many management consultants reading this will scoff and consider these ten-year statistics meager. They will take pride and honor in their numbers that dwarf these. These brags are common among consultants, and they are positively absurd.

Some travel stands out more than others. One Friday, I was asked to represent our firm in a twenty-person army of bankers, lawyers, private equity professionals, and rival consultants at a "management meeting" that was to begin the following Monday. Management meetings are where private equity leaders tell acquisition targets that they "have always loved their business" and that "we're different because we are in it for the long run." The consultant's role in these meetings is to convert the copious amounts of data and information into three questions to the acquisition target's CEO that make the consultants look smart in the eyes of the private equity leaders. The final decision to gather this group for the meeting happened on Saturday morning. Tickets were booked Saturday afternoon, and the delegates departed from their respective cities to the meeting location on Sunday night.

I should note that this particular meeting was taking place in Gold Coast, Australia. As each of us slept in our pods and wore the Qantas pajamas, the target company (a sports apparel brand that you know) decided to sell itself to another party, using our in-flight status as leverage. We heard the news shortly after landing. After a quick twenty-four hours enjoying the beach, I was back at the airport headed home to Dallas to receive my next assignment. I left for Australia on a Sunday night, landed on a Tuesday morning, departed at 1:00 p.m. on Thursday, and landed at noon on Thursday. It's the closest I've come to time travel.

Consulting firms primarily compensate for the travel absurdities, sleep deprivation, and nerve-frying pressures through lofty compensation packages. My first-year base salary comfortably had six digits. A few years later, I was fourteen questions deep into a game of *Who Wants to Be a Millionaire*. By the end, I was making more than the NFL and NBA league minimums of the time. It was a stupid amount of money. That I lived in a one-bedroom apartment in Uptown Dallas was a testament to the financial conservatism embedded in me early in life. I did buy a considerably ridiculous BMW M3 in an eye-popping shade of Carolina blue (specifically Yas Marina blue, for the fellow BMW color dorks) as an indulgence, but that was a rare lapse in my piggybank-filling process. Money didn't move my needle.

More motivating were the generous travel accommodations and boondoggles. For the most part, we flew in business class or better and stayed in top-tier hotels (except in far-reaching places where only a "lowly" Westin was available). We were allowed to use equivalent travel funds to fly somewhere other than home for the weekend, a perk that afforded the perpetual avoidance of reality and setting down roots. I used this hack to travel the world, catching up on the years that I missed out on globe-trotting.

While on the road with our teams (usually five to ten eager youngsters and a few project managers), we would plan events that ranged from luxurious steak dinners to F1 track racing to nights out in Vegas, even when Vegas wasn't anywhere close to the client site. I genuinely enjoyed and appreciated almost everyone I worked with. This was a group of smart and accomplished people, typically in their twenties and thirties, who generally were humble and wanted to do good work. To celebrate success with them seemed well-earned and a good use of time (and *not* client funds, which is a popular misconception).

Closer to home, the firm would also sponsor lavish and often spectacular internal events throughout the year to reward our work in "soft compensation." The social calendar looked roughly as follows:

Spring: Lunch upon dinner upon brunch upon campus visit to lure recruits to work at our firm to keep the high-turnover operation cranking; overselling the notion that they'd only work on world-changing, nonprofit climate change suppression and solving world hunger and downplaying organizational delayering work at aerospace companies.

Summer: An egregiously unrealistic representation of life working at our firm, with happy hours every Friday and elaborate outings every Saturday; an office-wide retreat in Austin where we take over a large resort and disrupt the leisure and peace of all unaffiliated hotel guests, always with a distinct costume party.

Fall: More recruiting locally and on campus to shower those with offers from the summer to sign up for the long haul, always bringing an offering of free food and logo paraphernalia.

Winter: The annual end-of-year holiday party, where we congratulate ourselves for our conquests of the high-end consulting market by distributing champagne, eating from chocolate fountains, and dancing as ineffectively as possible (side note: one time Chris Harrison from *The Bachelor* franchise attended this party, and it was the most dramatic shocking ending in holiday party history).

Between all the extracurriculars (and maybe because of them), the firm's global revenue and panache grew. Our firm, our office, and our practice grew like a mushroom. To this day, I maintain that I made the right choice of firm, and I guide my friends' younger siblings and kids to the consulting life. In spite of the pain that I felt, that firm and job yielded more personal growth than I could have accomplished anywhere else. I view this positivity in isolation from anything else that happened in the later years.

I started my full-time consulting career on September 29, 2008. I vowed to make it to two years. Two turned into three. Three turned into seven. Every year in that job was like three years in the "real world." The promises made to me from the individuals and the firm itself were coming true in terms of career success. Most importantly, the promotion path gave me all the sense of accomplishment I'd hoped to receive and all the validation that nobody could take from me. I did whatever it took to blur out the self-imposed pressure for perfection and the cracks it created.

I never imagined I would make it to the mythical partner level, but that's exactly what happened on July 1, 2016 (I was one of those three interns who made it; bet you never saw that coming). It was a validation of all of the output I created, the hours and miles I invested, and the trust built with the partnership that my contribution would create incremental equity value to the firm. I was granted citizenship among a population of brilliant strategists and practitioners, men and women who authored books and held court in boardrooms around the world.

I was a former fat kid who failed sixth grade and lost the middle school speech contest.

My peers who made the same cut of partner celebrated with champagne and feasts, boasted on social media with pomp and circumstance, and

This is what crippling self-doubt looks like in a stylish blazer basked in the glow of the worldwide email announcing the coronation of the new class of partners (I was among forty or so globally in my class).

I responded quite differently because my circumstances were very different from those of my peers. I was only promoted to partner because of who I knew, not the quality of work that I did, and every partner around the world was aware of that. Through a series of specific maneuvers by my supporters, I managed to sneakily clear every hurdle in the intricate election process. Even worse, *everyone* knew this—my peers and even junior staff members who worked for me. I was among the least intelligent people at the entire firm, let alone among the partnership. I was set up for failure. And when I did fail, instead of a simple and quiet "transition" in our up-or-out model, it would be a public, epic, and celebrated unraveling of the truth—that I didn't deserve to be a partner by any measure. I would never sell a project, I would be abandoned by my few supporters, and, worst of all, I would let down the partners who ushered me into this elite position.

Of course, none of this was true. I earned my gilded seat in the Hall of Partners as rightfully as any of my newly anointed colleagues. But that didn't stop me from a three-day alcohol binge to numb my unfounded shame and insecurity. A simple dinner with friends and a cheesy LinkedIn post would have been much better.

I was the little boy at the pool seeing his friends thrown around by the older kid. I was the fifth grader experiencing normal adolescent taunting by his acquaintances. There was nothing rational to my reaction to the stimulus placed in front of me, and it tortured me in the same way as when I was kid. This time, there was no school to which to transfer, no life to leave behind, no guardrails to keep me in my lanes. I had to find new ways to cope. I leaned into new people, practices, and compulsions that would ultimately lead me to some very bumpy roads and then to the edge of a cliff.

CHAPTER 17

DANGER ZONE

S enior-level management consultants often find themselves in odd situations and locations and among odd groups of people. For those like me who spent more than a little bit of their youth in a creek or a construction site, almost every situation has the potential for me to be a fish out of water. I've been in boardrooms with crying CEOs. I've chilled with country star Luke Bryan in the referee's dressing room at Madison Square Garden. I've stood at the podium of the White House press room (the one place where I didn't feel unqualified compared to others who have been there).

Hands down, the bougiest and most lavish setting in which I found myself happened at one of my first global partner conferences. This is the semi-annual event when a thousand millionaires get together in a single location to present the Instagram version of their work and to celebrate six months of client services triumph. The crown jewel of that week's gathering was a private gala held at the Louvre, which the firm had rented out entirely. The last time I was at this museum was as a backpacking tourist on a student discount card. This time, I held champagne as my colleagues and I roamed the halls and took selfies within inches of the Mona Lisa. I channeled my best Tom Cruise/Brian Flanagan from *Cocktail* to sarcastically review the art while holding my glass.

These classy affairs typically ended with factions splitting into numerous geographical and practice area cohorts at bars and clubs around the city. We rarely saw people with whom we worked so closely over the years and through the ranks, so when we did, we blew the doors off. After the Louvre, the attendees from my office and a few others swarmed booths at an exclusive, trendy, and terrible Parisian club. Bottles of Dom with glowing labels arrived continuously. We laughed, danced (horrifically), and ignored emails from our project teams working diligently back home in the US.

I ended that night stumbling down the Champs-Élysées at three in the morning. I learned the next day that I was being followed by some sketchy characters before I was saved and pulled into a cab. I remember very little. I woke up to texts from colleagues (many of whom were equally turned up) containing a mix of concern, confusion, and shame-inciting pictures and recaps of my words and actions. I had vague memories of an extremely tense conversation with someone; I think it was one of two people, but I'm still not sure. I missed my flight the next morning and barely got back for a wedding that I couldn't miss. I was physically sick, psychologically shaken, and horrified by my behavior in a catastrophized version of a half-remembered night. You'd think this would be a wake-up call, but it wasn't. This had happened many times before. I always moved past it, and I knew that at the next opportunity I'd probably do it all over again.

As a high-flying partner at a flashy management consultancy, I was a classic car, a beautiful 1968 Camaro with a sparkling blue paint job, turning heads and receiving thumbs-up signs from strangers on the sidewalk. Under the shiny sheet metal, the drivetrain was in shambles, and the frame was rotting from rust accumulated over decades of being exposed to elements. I was traveling on an increasingly rocky path and praying that the lug nuts would hold the wheels in place.

My consulting career has been an investment that paid off in multiple ways personally and professionally. I earned those returns at the expense of immeasurable comfort and peace of mind. It's not because the job or the lifestyle is inherently bad across the board. It's because the job and the lifestyle are not fit for every personality.

I have always been a homebody. I have always had severe anxiety with change. Among the worst nights of my life were those before starting a new school year or job. Blank slates were terror-inducing prospects. Now, management consulting is nothing but travel (four days a week on the road), constant change (clients, managers, responsibilities), and blank slates (every project had a stand-alone performance evaluation; every promotion had a new scorecard). Add to that the fact that my brain couldn't process stimuli properly. I bent my true self to fit the mold of a perfect consultant, which was immeasurably painful and unsustainable. Success and enrichment in the job were underdogs in this game.

For ten years, I twisted and contorted myself into a person who could manage these stressors. I shoved all of my anxiety to the bottom drawer. I miserably packed a suitcase every Sunday night while ignoring the weeknight good times, ball games, and dates that normal people enjoyed. I powered through the fear of failure in the eyes of unfamiliar project managers, partners, and client executives. I acted stoic and talked tough. This charade was all for the promise of stellar performance evaluations and (strategically-timed-for-retention) promotions that yielded more responsibility and status. And yes, more money, too, but I never actually considered that as a factor—which I understand is a very privileged and easy thing to say when you're making a lot of it.

A well-established misconception is that these strains begin to ease once you make partner. But if you've ever been skiing, you know what it's like to ride the chairlift to what you *think* is the summit of the mountain until you crest the visual peak and see that you're merely halfway to the apex. It was the same with partnership at the firm where I worked—there are multiple degrees of partner and a new set of pressures burdened onto our backs at mid-mountain. The idea that a partner is like a tenured professor is not true. Continued success and elevation to higher altitudes required dogged labor and relentless commercial hunting, all while receiving none of the plaudits rained down upon the more fragile and less enriched junior staff. Said another way, nobody feels sorry for people who make that much money. I faked it 'til I made it; then when I "made it," the climb only got harder. The mismatch between my expectations and reality became more pronounced.

The obvious question is: if money wasn't that important and the job was twisting me to a breaking point, then why did I keep doing it? That would have been a valid query three promotions earlier, let alone seven years in. I persevered to show my dad how successful I had become, that I was a son he could brag about. He could put his hand on my shoulder and tell me how proud he was and that he knew all along that I'd thrive in my career. I looked forward to the day we would sit on a dock at Lake Norman, maybe the one we went to when I was a kid, and, over a beer, we'd talk business and the spoils of a life well lived. All of that would be reward enough.

It had been ten years since his funeral. His status at the time remained "deceased." It was a conundrum.

In spite of his continued lack of breathing and earthly existence, I kept pushing harder. Failure was not an option, and neither was genuine appreciation from the source that mattered most. Therefore, I sought validation, distraction, and medication to fuel my ambition and anesthetize my aches from being a try-hard.

Extravagant, high-profile concerts and sporting events became increasingly affordable and accessible channels to replenish the spirit. They provided a like-minded community and positive anticipation of showtime and kickoff. Even in the agony of defeat (Panthers fans unite), there is support and commiseration.

The cost and time commitment of sporting events and concerts accelerated parallel to my titles and stress levels in my career. In the first half of 2016, I attended the Super Bowl, the Final Four, and the Kentucky Derby (bad luck fact: the Panthers, the Tar Heels, and the horse on which I wagered all finished in second place). On consecutive nights in a single weekend in the summer I made partner, I saw Bruce Springsteen in Gothenburg, Sweden, and Guns N' Roses in Washington, DC. Seeing my sixty-third Bruce Springsteen show and witnessing a reunion of my favorite band, both within a thirty-six-hour period, should have sent me to peak euphoria. Instead, I was mired in self-doubt and uncertainty regarding my newly attained partner status during both concerts. Joy was stolen.

I coped with the unpredictable and stressful nature of my life by taking control of anything I could. This included obsessing over my weight. We've established that I was a fat kid growing up. We don't need to revisit that. I can provide photos. There's no need for photos.

I became un-fat for the first time in high school. I became re-fat in college. I became un-fat and stayed that way until I started my consulting job. Hundred-hour weeks, life on the road, and unlimited food and beverage budgets inflated me to full Violet Beauregarde status, minus the blue hue. From 2008 to 2010 (my late twenties), I went from Elvis Presley on the Ed Sullivan Show to Elvis Presley in his residency at the International Hotel in Las Vegas. If Neil Armstrong saw my face, he'd probably try to land on it. I think I've made my point; I was a big dude.

On January 1, 2010, I made the decision to stop being extra-husky for good. I strapped on some lightly used running shoes and hit the sidewalk for a jiggly, joint-jolting, half-mile run. I looked like Rerun chasing after the pickup truck in the opening sequence of *Good Times*. (I'm reaching pretty deep here, I know; just look it up on YouTube.) The next day, I ran a little farther before dry heaving. By the end of January, I was able to run two miles without interruption. I was hooked on the sense of accomplishment, so I set an ambitious goal to run a 10K by the end of the year.

I paired this slow running with more sensible eating, which started to pay dividends for my waistline and my scale, both of which had been screaming for mercy. I lost five pounds, and my buttons relaxed a bit. Five pounds became ten. Ten became twenty. The "hey, you look different" and "you used to be fatter" comments started to roll in. They were shots of validation delivered straight into my veins. I looked and felt better. The attention and compliments went from drip to firehose as the weight continued to melt away.

Runs stretched to five miles long by late February. In July, I ran a 10K. By December, I finished a half marathon in under two hours.

In just under one year, I lost seventy pounds (more than a fourth of my body weight) and ran 690.1 miles. The next year, I ran 1,026.5

miles, including a step-up to the full Dallas Marathon. I do not recommend marathons to anybody. It was the single worst physical experience of my life. I was built for comfort, not for delivering news to Athens that Greece won a battle. I continued to run until recently, when my Achilles tendon decided that my running career was over.

Attending meaningful and high-profile events and pursuing fitness are honorable and productive activities. They are healthy outlets, until they aren't. I left out a few parts.

I missed events with friends and family (and even some work obligations) to go to concerts and games. And let me repeat, I went to *sixty-three* Bruce Springsteen concerts. I appreciate all of them, but I probably could have cut a few. I was chasing songs, setlists, and feelings of exuberance and connection I couldn't replicate elsewhere in my real life. When Springsteen tours ended, I would become legitimately sad. I would endlessly relisten to concerts and watch videos deep into the night to try to recapture some of the spirit.

I lost those seventy pounds in only four months. I would go days eating only small cups of Frosted Mini-Wheats. When work hours ran long and prohibited normal morning or evening runs, I would pound out four or five miles at two in the morning so I wouldn't miss a day. Multiple people pulled me aside to ask if I had an eating disorder. Until a few months ago, I weighed myself up to ten times a day. An unfavorable number on the scale materially affected my mood and how I presented myself to others. Running and weight loss wasn't a health mission—it was a compulsion and an addiction.

My most destructive self-medication came in a more traditional form. In the spring of my junior year of high school, my good friend and I visited his sister at Duke University. She was in her first year of college, having recently elevated from high school goddess status. She brought an unsuspecting roommate to our dinner at Torero's Mexican Restaurant in Durham, North Carolina, to witness my first dance with alcohol (save for those Coors Light sips my dad gave me as a toddler). For my heretofore teetotaling self, it was like picking up a basketball for the first time and going one-on-one with Charles Oakley. The giant, overly tequila'd pitcher of house margarita was far stronger than me and had no regard for my well-being. Within a little over an hour, I'd experienced my first taste of liquor, my first buzz, and my first "brownout" (the lights went dim for a few minutes over refried beans and Mexican rice).

My second drinking experience was the following summer, incidentally with the same people, and involved a keg stand during which I was dropped on my collarbone. I spent the next week at my dad's family beach trip with an inexplicable and disgusting bruise between my neck and left shoulder. My third drinking experience included consuming mystery punch at a terrible fraternity party during the UNC orientation. That night ended with me getting lost on my walk back to the dorm, followed by a day-long hangover.

With my early track record of drinking, you might think I would have learned my lesson. And actually, I did. Save for a few youthful and moronic moments of overconsumption, I spent most of college and my early twenties with a relatively low regard for alcohol. It was always present, and I certainly indulged, but it existed to make a good time a little better.

The role of alcohol changed as I veered further from my true, guardrail-contained self to the distorted version that sought career conformity and accomplishment. I used alcohol to numb the mental and emotional soreness of job stress, fuel the engine to gain social and romantic validation, and salve the guilt and shame from my behavior while under the influence. It was a horrific and vicious cycle that seemed difficult to escape.

Alcohol was ever-present both culturally and logistically in my life. At work, there was never a shortage of alcohol, whether it was stocked at a planned office event or in the form of a limitless bar tab. Drinking and debauchery were encouraged and seemingly rewarded. Networking and bonding happened over bottles of Blue Label and shots of Patrón. Fine wine drinkers (not me) chuckled as ludicrously expensive bottles arrived at the dinner table, for little reason other than it was possible. Recruiting events would often devolve into bottle service at a nearby club, even for those of us who were too old to be there. We had beer and wine in our office with loose rules of consumption, enabling a 3:00 p.m. start on Fridays. (It was not unusual to still be at the office until late at night on Fridays—not because there was work to do but because the booze was on the house.) It was debauchery, it was fun, and it was dysfunctional.

To be extra clear, I do not lay any blame for what happened to me on the availability of alcohol at work events. I do recognize now that it was a challenging enabler for people in my situation—those who use alcohol as a numbing agent for the invisible strains and cracks from the job. I hear that the firm has dialed down the alcohol at events. I think that's a good thing.

It didn't feel like alcohol was a problem for me. I was not a drink-before-work, never-sober-for-a-moment alcoholic. But that didn't make me less of an abuser. Alcohol went from something that *added joy to an existing good time* to something I utilized to *create a good time* to medicine that *numbed a bad time*. That was when the trouble reached guy-in-a-spiral-montage levels. Hangovers were beginning to impact productivity at home and at work. I gained weight, which ignited crippling self-loathing. With greater frequency, I was waking up with the terrible mystery of "what did I do?" and "what did I say?" regarding the night before. More often than before, I had a reason to be embarrassed by my words and actions. Admonishments and apologies became routine. The shame and guilt compounded.

The charade that I was able to manage the inner storm of my psychological struggles while looking the part of a partner came to a crashing halt in the summer of 2018. On a Friday in July, I gave a presentation in our London office, the timing of which coincided with a particularly tumultuous and stressful point in my partner tenure. I was having a knockout year of revenue production, which, in the business model of my practice area, meant I was working on six or seven simultaneous client efforts. That meant six or seven times the number of demanding clients, six or seven times the number of cities, and six or seven times the typical amount of imposter syndrome and fear of failure that I typically maintained.

On the evening after my presentation, there was a very glamorous party on top of a luxurious high rise, teeming with consultants cutting loose and celebrating their awesomeness. Of course there were several well-stocked and well-staffed bars pouring generously. As a guest, who was I to turn down some drinks? Humming with the energy of the crowd, the admiration of a performance well received, and the insatiable devil of self-punishment inside me, I pushed the limits of how much I could drink and be Mr. Fun Pants without crossing the line of decorum. Whether I crossed it or not is something I can't tell you. At some point in the night, I failed to be a reliable narrator of my own experience.

Shortly after my return stateside, the judgment that I had gone too far was made for me. On a Friday, I received an email to report to our office on Saturday morning. When I arrived, I saw my partner sponsor and the head of our region sitting silently and sternly. They wasted no time in telling me that I was being terminated. The liability of out-of-control Michael outweighed the benefit I was providing.

I didn't panic. My heart didn't sink. My stomach didn't twist, and my blood pressure remained steady as their words sunk in. My first reaction was relief. I had spent years running into a fog knowing that, at some point, I'd reach a cliff over which I would teeter. I had finally found it, and I was forced to face the fall. I had been warned. I had been admonished. And I hadn't stopped running.

I spent the next twenty minutes asking questions. Most of them were logical—how to wind down my involvement in our work, how severance worked, when I would clean out my office and say goodbye (or if I was even allowed to). The bearers of the news were gentlemen and treated me with dignity and respect. They were particularly gracious in letting me leave that room quickly when the dump truck of reality hit my heart. That "I'm about to sneeze" feeling hit as I considered losing my friends, my identity, and the work into which I had poured the whole of my mind, heart, and body. I proudly fought off tears until I slinked out of the building and into a world that no longer looked the same.

I immediately went to a workout class. I went to lunch with my friend. I went home and stared at the wall. I called my mentee Sam to tell him the news and bawled like a baby. I went to my friend's to drink Coors (Banquet, not Light) while watching *Smokey and the Bandit*. I numbly fell asleep to face the next day's uncertainty. I will never forget these details.

For weeks, I was filled with a complex cocktail of emotions. I was angry at those who reported concerns about my behavior to the powers that be. I was angry at myself because it was hard to defend my position—I *was* drinking too much and sometimes *was* too much to handle. I was scared for what the future held.

Above all, I was ashamed—ashamed of what people would think of me and ashamed for failing every person and institution that believed in me. In my irrational, anxious mind, I pictured breaking news tweets from the accounts of CNN, Fox News, and the nonexistent Elite Management Consulting and Senior Executive News Network reporting my demise.

Shame is a self-imposed feeling, and it is a bear. It doesn't go away without hard and purposeful work. I would later learn how to ease that monster. At the time, it was all-consuming and invincible.

Towering above all of the aforementioned sources of self-loathing was this: I heard some people reporting that I made them uncomfortable while drunk. This generated the most shame (and still does). Anyone who truly knows me would (probably . . . hopefully?) agree that I do not wish people harm physically or emotionally. I suppose alcohol birthed and nurtured a negative being inside of me, like how water turns one of those little pills into a foamy dinosaur. As I became more tenured and kept attending the boozy work events, I never considered myself anything but one of the fun and young members of the crew. I understand now that even a positively intended comment or an inquiry about a twenty-two-year-old staff member, female or male, can be interpreted as an advance or a threat when the source is a drunk six-foot-four person of titular influence.

Like a *Bachelorette* contestant not receiving a rose in the ceremony, in December 2018, I took a moment and said my goodbyes. I broke the news of my exit to colleagues and clients, including many close friends who I know now I'd never see or talk to again. I never knew who knew the real story of why I was leaving. As I understand it, a few people did at the time, and most knew within a few months. Now, I guess everyone knows. I am tired of running from that truth; I feel liberated in writing these words.

It was Christmastime. I hid the details of my "career change" from my friends and family. They kept congratulating me for taking such a bold step, for wrenching control of my life from a job that was owning me. I received admiration from all around for being brave. I was a fraud. I felt ashamed. I put on a mask, recited all of the ex-consultant bumper stickers ("It was time for me to move to the client side"; "I am looking for a more sustainable lifestyle"; "I didn't like this season's logo vests") and kept moving.

At church on Christmas Eve, I thought about how the experience and loss could potentially be a blessing and not even one in disguise. You might think that getting fired from a job that meant everything to me would be enough to encourage a large-scale change. You would be wrong.

CHAPTER 18

HERE I GO AGAIN

I advise caution when enabling uncensored, anonymous, and public question-and-answer sessions while striving for ultimate transparency in front of your new team of 150 people. Be particularly prudent when you are the newly named head of a function in which you have absolutely no expertise. This was my exact situation shortly into my tenure at my post-consulting job working for a multibillion-dollar restaurant company. After a leadership shake-up, the CEO bestowed upon me the hallowed honor of being at the helm of the information technology function.

For those not familiar with the role of IT in a company, here you go: just as you don't thank and praise the toilet each time it properly flushes, the technology professionals are never thanked when the computer works properly. But just as you scream and curse at the toilet for not disposing of waste as designed, the IT department takes a strong kick to the nether regions when there's a glitch in a printer.

The crowd in that conference room seemed skeptical of my selection as head of IT, as they should have been. The extent of my technology repair skills was limited to unplugging and replugging the device and blowing into it like a Nintendo console. After a brief introduction and gracious handing over of the keys from the outgoing leader, the question-and-answer session began. The first question was a flaming hot missile: "Do you have any IT experience or certifications?"

Silence and regret for this forum hung over me as I searched my brain for a vague and reasonable answer. Instead, I looked inward and thought about the intersection of what was true and empathetic to this group. I told them I had none whatsoever. I assured them it was a good thing—they wouldn't have someone looking over their shoulder critiquing their work. I asked them for patience and grace as they taught me information and processes. I informed them of my skill set in identifying issues and prioritizing solutions and promised them that I would be their advocate on the executive team. I would fight for resources and represent our interests.

I never thought I would be an IT executive, nor did I expect any CEO in their right mind to select me to be one. I will forever cherish my time in that role. The people on that team worked harder and more humbly than anyone I had encountered before them. We shared a lot of laughs, even in times of misery—including (and especially) during all the late nights we spent praying and holding our breath that our rickety online ordering system would withstand the weekend crush. More than once, I was moved to tears as I regaled the executive group with heroic tales of the IT team's technical ingenuity and dogged perseverance to support our business. Looking back, I probably showed too much emotion.

I also became an effective business leader by using three questions:

1. What does this thing do?
2. How much does it cost?
3. What happens if we don't have it?

Armed with these three simple queries, one can go far without a shred of functional expertise.

My unlikely path to the mighty seat of IT overlord began with an unexpected phone call only a few months after the tumultuous end of my consulting career. The CEO of a former client had a short-term need and asked if I could work my consulting magic independently. I said yes, so I worked up an elite-sounding firm name (Winwood Collins LLC, named after the dad-rock scions Steve and Phil) and got to work. That gig turned out to be an extended interview, which yielded an offer to join in a very senior executive role.

The opportunity to be a chief something-or-another at a huge public company was quite intriguing and tempting. After enduring a turbulent decade, I made a pledge to continue my career with a job that met a set of guidelines that I believed would lead to better outcomes. I was determined to make selecting a job easy by comparing the attributes of the role in question with an objective, concrete rubric:

Job attributes for a healthier Michael		Job attributes for role at hand
Move closer to home and family	→	In Tampa where I knew nobody
Work in an industry I'm passionate about	→	Went to an industry that didn't excite me
Lead a function I love and in which I'm an expert	→	In charge of several functions in which I had no experience or interest
Develop and grow a team	→	Cut substantial cost and head count
De-emphasize financial compensation as a critical attribute	→	Higher pay than consulting job, compensation was public knowledge
Limited alcohol occasions and emphasis	→	Closet full of liquor around the corner, kegerator next to my office
Work with people I like and respect	→	Team of people I liked and respected

And thus, consistent with so many other completely irrational decisions of the era, I accepted the job that met only one of my seven criteria. I made a 14.3 percent good choice.

Over the past few years, I had made bold proclamations and taken concrete steps to "hit the reset button" while I was descending into greater struggles with my delusions, anxieties, and self-medications. I would get a new car, move apartments, or change my regular seat in first class on American Airlines and expect that my life would magically transform. My move to Tampa and into a completely new profession was supposed to be the ultimate transformation, the be-all and end-all of metamorphosis that would surely turn my life around. I decided that I wouldn't hesitate to set down roots and enjoy the spoils of being a consulting graduate with a big, fancy corporate job.

I bought a big South Tampa house near the water with a pool and three more bedrooms than there were occupants. I fully furnished it immediately, in the hopes that a family would grow into it in the coming years. I bought a Jeep for top-down, sand-in-my-toes drives from the beach. I was fortunate to get plugged into a social scene and friends with country club memberships. I believed I was on a path to the good, adult life with a family and a stable foundation.

My new job was a bright spot in my life, at least for the first several months. I loved leading my team and having an impact on our company. I enjoyed being out in the restaurants, engaging with the employees and the customers. It was fulfilling to have a seat at the table in shaping brands I loved and to create better customer experiences. One day six months in, I found myself walking into work smiling. I hadn't traveled in weeks. I was working reasonable hours. I believed I had the respect and admiration of my team and my colleagues. I couldn't believe how happy I was, and I was skeptical about whether it would last.

It did not last. The longer-term weathering effects of a permanent lifestyle change began to create cracks. I remained well outside of my guardrails, without close friends or family members nearby. I was haunted by ever-present and growing pain, shame, and guilt from a previous life and some bad habits that I couldn't shake. I continued to grieve for stable, nuclear family happiness (both my own family of origin and the idea of a wife and kids). I turned forty on a Wednesday in August 2019. I took inventory of my life and did not like the collection of circumstances.

The nature of my work was also far more anxiety-inducing than I expected. In addition to overseeing several large-scale, resume-building technology rollouts, I was also asked to substantially reduce the workforce that I inherited. I knew that layoff conversations were part of being a senior executive. Incidentally, I have become very good at them, but it is not a skill I have ever aspired to attain. I will now fire you:

- Hey, reader. Thanks for coming in today.
- There are a lot of changes happening today.
- I wanted to tell you as soon as I could that your role has been eliminated.
- I really appreciate all the work you've done.
- Now here's Jennie from HR to tell you all the stuff I don't want to tell you.

Boom. Thirty seconds, and my job is done.

As a lifelong people-pleaser and anti-confrontation all-star, the idea of these conversations was daunting. The horrific nature of repeatedly snuffing out good people's sources of income became a burden that I had to keep inside. Nobody feels sorry for the person whose princely salary is printed in public documents, even if that person dies a little on the inside ninety times over a two-year period. Sixty of those moments came all at once when I outsourced three teams in a five-minute Zoom call. It was an agonizing move, a piercingly sad moment, and entirely necessary to do over virtual space given the health protocols in 2020. That moment created a step change in my mental state.

Pain management in the consulting days was as easy as jumping on a no-cost-to-me international flight and taking in a Guns N' Roses show or partying with work colleagues in an exotic locale. Not only did my new lifestyle not afford such distractions, but there was also a global issue that prevented sporting events and concerts. I'm not sure how much you watched the news in 2020 and 2021, but there was actually a rather large-scale global health crisis that prohibited large crowds from gathering. I would never begin to place full responsibility for my issues on a pandemic, but it didn't help.

Separation from friends and loved ones made those Zoom happy hours socially acceptable and drinking alone a stigma-free activity. I took that nugget of permission and turned it into a rotisserie chicken of solo intoxication. I made a rule for myself that I would only drink solo before I was going to dinner or when I got home from social outings. That meant that I could start drinking at four in the afternoon, go to dinner for an hour at seven, and then come home and finish off a few more until I couldn't sit up any longer. I had friends; I went out plenty. But I began loving the moments alone more than the dates and the parties.

Alcohol, the intended soother of guilt and shame, became a source of incremental embarrassment and indignity. The negative cycle began to spin into category five magnitudes, with Sunday's alcohol covering for Saturday's binge. Over the fall of 2021 and the winter of 2022, the pattern escalated and reached a head to the point of endangering myself and others. Run-of-the-mill drinking escalated to some serious incidents.

On a Saturday in the fall, after a day of considerable beer guzzling and golfing on a guys' weekend, I dimwittedly concluded that it would be safe to drive a short distance from the course clubhouse to our rented residence in a private, gated neighborhood. With the fat-fingered clumsiness of a tipsy, sunburned golf hack, I accidentally disabled traction control while starting the car. When I hit the gas on a left turn, I may as well have been on ice; we skidded at a measly eighteen miles per hour into a dinky lamp post that crumbled like a soccer player tapped with a pinkie finger. The impact left a nasty dent in the hood, though the car remained drivable. My friend (who was riding shotgun) and I cruised back to the house, parked the car in the garage, and hoped nobody would notice a trail of oil leading to a garage hiding a banged-up supercar.

Four hours later, I met a nice police officer who was tipped off by neighborhood security who had witnessed the incident. He ticketed me for reckless driving and leaving the scene but was unable to charge me with a DUI without account of any drinking in the time between the wreck and our conversation.

I was relieved, embarrassed, and terrified by the prospect of what could have happened. What if it had been a person and not a lamp post? What if it had been fifty miles per hour and not eighteen? What if my passenger had been injured? I could have killed myself or someone else or gone to prison and ruined my life. I would not do well in prison. I tried hard to chalk up the accident to non-alcohol-related equipment issues and pilot error, but I couldn't shake the feeling that it could have been so tragic. In horrific irony, only alcohol could soothe the terrible imagery as I concocted mental scenarios of doom.

My struggle to stay above water amid whitecaps of anxiety, guilt, and self-loathing contributed to the demise of my status as a C-suite executive. By late 2021, my focus had become inordinately inward rather than stoking my own long-term career progression. Literal hangovers, my hangxiety (that awful feeling of not knowing what I said or did on a given night), and managing my personal relationships so distorted my career vision that I essentially fired myself from a perfectly good, very well-compensated role.

The short version is that the CEO made a smart organizational change that would take me out of my IT and digital leadership role and appoint me president of a business unit. As I look at it today from outside of my warped-at-the-time vision, it was a perfect opportunity to build my skill set and attain the credibility required to one day be a CEO. I would earn the same wage, gain invaluable experience, and tap into skills I actually enjoyed using instead of managing technology.

Instead, I funneled the anger, frustration, and paranoia erupting from my own mental state and behaviors into a conspiratorial victim narrative. I convinced myself that a few people inside the company were undermining and emasculating me. They believed I was incompetent and threatening, that I deserved to have my job taken from me and to be shoved into a corner. I would never succeed there, and they'd make sure I wouldn't thrive anywhere else.

Of course, none of that was true. The CEO is a good man who had my best long-term interest at heart, or at least in balance with the needs of the business. Other players were thinking of how best to operate our business and did not revel in my failure. In reality, I was failing myself in the broader context of my life, and I didn't want to admit it. Instead, it felt easier to blame an outside force; it created a shield of misery and disdain that deflected from my own reality.

On the outside, my disguise was indeed brilliant. Few recognized the seams bursting underneath the surface. To the surprise of many, I abruptly left the company in December 2021. It was my "I'll show you" moment that only demonstrated my instability. My unchecked psychological deterioration and subsequent self-medication tanked a second prestigious job in a three-year span. You might think that my malfunctioning mind encouraging me to foolishly leave a lucrative job would be enough to bring about a large-scale change. You would be wrong.

It's not much fun to recount the subsequent handful of months. It's also rather difficult to do because blackouts became more regular. I had a very embarrassing moment in my front yard when a neighbor reminded me of a very long visit I'd had with him and his wife the weekend before. I had no recollection, and he caught on. In Las Vegas, I would wake up with no memory of how I got from dinner on one end of the strip to my bed on the other end. Being a pedestrian in Vegas is like walking an *American Ninja Warrior* course with obstacles of danger and debauchery—and this is when sober, let alone when recently drowned in brown liquor. I experienced multiple mornings of reaching out to friends I was with the night before, cringing while I asked what I'd said and done. Eventually this cost me companions who had long stayed by my side but who gave up on making sense of me. My relationships crumbled. Isolation crept in.

As the college basketball season approached March Madness, I was physically and mentally exhausted from keeping up the boozy charade that I was doing fine, that I had control. I threw everything I had at keeping myself above water—increasing the frequency and volume of drinking, seeking attention and validation at all costs, and taking trips to basketball games made possible by the Tar Heels' unlikely run through the NCAA tournament. I even resorted to jumping back into high-pressure job opportunities, going through a few job interview processes and getting to the altar with one. The ball was in my court to become the chief operating officer of a restaurant company you've probably heard of. It was a big opportunity, and I couldn't make a clear decision in the tumult of my psychological state.

The hope of finding happiness faded, as all of my go-to medications only hurt me worse. I stopped sleeping well. Working out became a rarity. I wasn't eating right. I withdrew from my friends and family. I wondered if I was reaching my Nicolas Cage *Leaving Las Vegas* moment.

In late March, on the eve of the UNC-inclusive Final Four, I poured my broken soul and bloated body into that rented Ford Mustang where I thought about ending it all. A twice-self-destructed, shamed client services leader and corporate executive with no place to go. My once-bustling inbox was gone. My Outlook calendar was empty. Nobody called for my opinion on a business matter. When my friends expressed concern, I retorted with faux stability.

The cycle of recklessly hunting for validation and dousing my fires with alcohol became unsustainable. I concluded there was no graceful way to undo all of the damage I had created in my own life and others' without facing shame-soaked consequences. The only clean way out would be headlights-first into a ditch. Thank God that I had a burst of clarity and that my mother answered the phone that night. Thank God my sister came to be at my side. Thank God for the mindfulness that I needed to stop my life and seek intensive, inpatient help.

CHAPTER 19

MAN IN THE MIRROR

The insecure overachiever has the ultimate love-hate relationship with evaluation. We absolutely love filling our bottomless reservoir of validation with positive feedback. We also do not accept said positive feedback. We assume that it is a function of luck, someone else's misfortune, or a setup for future disaster. We lose all of our warm fuzzy feelings when we are hit with the "areas for development." We become Sonic the Hedgehog losing his coins, on his back watching his precious accolades fly away. And yet we continue to seek more opportunities for feedback so we can do it all over again.

Such was my feeling on my second-to-last day in the clinic, when I received my formal diagnoses. In an hour-long grand-finale session, each patient sat on the semi-comfortable couch of the visitors' room surrounded by their primary clinicians and caregivers. Also invited was the family member each patient chose to take along for the ride, so Elizabeth was dialed into a conference call. My psychologist, psychiatrist, social worker, and addiction specialist surrounded me in a semicircle, ready to unload their professional assessments and recommendations. I've never sat in front of a jury waiting to hear a verdict, but I have to think this was a close feeling.

An odd inner debate had been brewing for days leading up to that hearing. On the one hand, I didn't want to be saddled with a set of grim diagnoses and arduous follow-up therapies. I also didn't want them to find that nothing was seriously wrong with me and thus seemingly delegitimize my severe crisis mode and my admission weeks earlier. Plus, my friends in my cohort had shared their diagnoses with me, and I was bizarrely competitive about wanting to "beat" them with some doozies of my own.

The mood was heavy, but the love in the room was palpable. It was the first time I had heard Elizabeth's voice in conjunction with the professionals in the room. My home world and my protective bubble were colliding in a meeting that was all about me. The energy of the moment hit me hard, and I got that shaky-lip, feels-like-you're-gonna-sneeze feeling when you could cry at any moment. And cry I did when the psychologist kicked off the meeting by recounting my life story in deep detail. All the good, all the destructive, and all the hurdles and ziplines that he believed had led to my destination inside those walls. I suppose it's how Pee-wee Herman felt at the drive-in theater when he watched James Brolin and Morgan Fairchild portray his "Big Adventure" on the movie screen. I had lived the melodrama he described, but it felt like a reading of a Wikipedia entry of someone else's life. He and others in the room validated that, indeed, I had experienced a rough road even amid a privileged life.

It went something like this:

- Born with an underlying physiological brain chemistry thing (I'm not a doctor).
- Parents divorce and shake my foundation.
- Parents split across states, challenging my sense of security.
- Unchecked anxiety and perceived lack of security lead to irrational fear, withdrawal, and shame in elementary school.
- Total inability to self-validate, exacerbated by lack of direct validation from father.
- Really bad prom (this was not part of the evaluation; it's just worth mentioning).

- Dad dies; a source of potential validation disappears, and the guardrails on my life crumble.

- Life becomes dedicated to seeking validation professionally and socially at all costs.

- Ridiculously demanding and counter-to-my-needs management consulting career identified as a solution to validation requirements, which inflames underlying mental health challenges.

- Alcohol-fueled behavior to gain social validation exacerbates anxiety and depression; more alcohol then eases that shame and anxiety; round and round we go.

- Vicious cycle strengthens and accelerates, with the breaking point reached after second job crash.

- UNC defeats Duke in the 2022 NCAA Men's Basketball Final Four (this was not part of the evaluation; it's just worth mentioning).

- During a horrific meltdown, suicide becomes a viable option; inpatient mental health facility entered; life saved.

There are obviously so many positive bullet points that could be added to that list. But that wasn't the order of the day. That hour was about distilling forty-two years of disparate experiences into an explanatory narrative. I was glad that part was over.

I'm not going to recount all the diagnoses that came out of the doctors' mouths because that would be infringing on the duties of an actual medical professional who can properly describe them. I'll put it this way: there were a few components related to my physiological starting point at birth and a number of contributors from exogenous factors that happened to me. Think of it as three Reese's Peanut Butter Cups in the left hand (physical) and a collection of Skittles in the right hand (experiential). Mix them together, and it's both bad for you and really, really gross.

At a high level, my diagnosis was in the neighborhood of chronic and occasionally severe depression and some behavioral disorders that had tied a hand behind my back when it came to coping with the world.

It was a dossier that gave me street cred on the unit and hope for recovery and maintenance with medications and therapy.

All the behaviors I'd hated, feelings I'd feared, and irrational beliefs I'd had were a product of DNA and countless moments large and small. Now they had names. Now I knew what to fight. Now I knew it wasn't my fault.

Above all else I heard in that hour, I was most intrigued by the relationship between the timing of my "lowercase 't' traumas" (the doctors' clinical term) and the bizarre coping mechanisms I developed in my adult life. For years leading up to my check-in, I had compulsively listened to songs and watched music videos from the mid-to-late 1980s. I had incessantly and repeatedly watched contemporaneous movies. I even watched YouTube videos from those years, be it television commercials, sitcom introductions, or old newscasts. A particular favorite has been some dude's first-person camcorder footage of Charlotte that replicates a driver's point of view in 1987 (it's unbelievable how much of that content exists for what seems to be an audience of one psychologically scrambled man). My YouTube algorithm is like that of a time traveler. It's probably why I get a lot of ads for incontinence medications.

Consumption of digitized vintage content almost always accompanied heavy drinking. A typical cycle would be early evening viewings of Guns N' Roses and Metallica videos to get pumped up and buzzed. After a night out, I'd bring out the big guns—Madonna, Crowded House, Pet Shop Boys, and The Bangles. Each of these bands served the task of managing specific micro-emotions that came to the surface over the course of the night. On particularly rough nights, I'd dip further back into the early 1980s with some traditional yacht rock: "Key Largo," "I Keep Forgettin'," and "Even the Nights Are Better," played at window-rattling volumes, making me the only person who received complaints from neighbors for playing Air Supply and Bertie Higgins too loudly.

Guns N' Roses and Bruce Springsteen concerts have been my perpetual lifeboats in turbulent weather. *Appetite for Destruction* was released in 1987. Bruce Springsteen's four-cassette live opus was released in 1986. I bought it in 1987.

The era-specific intoxication wasn't limited to pop culture. I also had a long-standing habit of sifting through drawers of old belongings and pictures from that very specific age. I would also find myself lingering in front of 811 Museum Drive (my birth home) and 3810 Ayscough Road (the post-parental divorce home into which we moved in 1986) on visits to Charlotte. I'm sure the current residents thought I was casing the homes, and maybe it would have been worse if they actually knew that I was trying to see inside and add some concrete details to my memories.

Clearly, I had become obsessed with 1986 and 1987. I was sevenish. While at the clinic, I learned that most people begin to form more permanent personas and viewpoints on the world that age. It also happened to be when the world was changing around Elizabeth and me. You may remember that we coped with the change and the traumas, like our dad leaving, by sitting in the rec room and watching MTV. We had the liberty to watch movies that we shouldn't have. I played my Bruce Springsteen tapes to keep a connection between my dad and me alive.

For decades, I have coped with the pain of my existing life and longed for another life in the same way I had coped with longing for my old life on Museum Drive.

It makes sense now. I know it's unhealthy. Changes are necessary. I cannot keep living in the past and expect to move forward. Indulging in places, songs, and movies keeps the wounds open. I like to feel the pain of being in the shoes of the kid in the rec room, maybe because it feels like a way to change what happened over the next thirty-five years. But it has to stop; I have to give up the binging.

In numerous individual and group sessions, our facilitators used the phrase "catch it and change it." Be it a thought, behavior, or compulsion, our challenge was to identify spins into the irrational or repetitive and find an alternative behavior that would break the cycle. In my case, it was applicable to a number of themes, thoughts, and actions.

Catch it	→	Change it
I'm a broken mess	→	I have real and valid reasons for being the way I am
If only the past was different	→	I'll make great decisions in my control today
After all that hard work, I've ultimately failed in my career	→	After all that hard work, I know what to look for next in my career
Let's get drunk and forget all of the above	→	How about a head-clearing bike ride instead?
Fire up that "Paradise City" video!	→	Good idea (but only once in a while)

I wish I'd had the strength, wherewithal, and encouragement to catch and change my psychological patterns earlier. I encourage anyone who relates to some of these patterns to act sooner rather than later. Small seeds blossom into life-stifling weeds. It's better to cull them early and preventatively. And if someone in your life is stuck, give them a nudge.

Keep an especially close watch on those listening to too much Whitesnake.

CHAPTER 20

DON'T DREAM IT'S OVER

Journal entry: Wednesday, May 18, 2022

It's coming to an end

Another goodbye ceremony tonight. I'm up next

It's coming to an end

The emotions are stacking up

Sadness, grief, anticipation, pride, uncertainty, so many

But the time is coming

Enjoy the moment

You'll dream about it later

You're in the place you'll dream about

Can't come back

Won't come back

It'll all be a memory

I do my best to soak in moments that I know I'll look back on. It started when I was in graduate school, living a carefree life in a beautiful city where I'd never live again. I would stand in the living room, look out the tenth-floor window at the otherworldly frozen Lake Michigan, and tell myself, "In a few months, you'll wish you were here again because your life will be miserable in your first year of management consulting, so you'd better appreciate this while it lasts."

My sentiment in the final days of my psych ward stay was not about comparing the moment against future agony. It was about appreciating a time and place that I would never forget, one that changed me as a person and revealed what I wanted for the second half of my life. There were friends I would miss, peace for which I knew I'd long, and routine for which I would pine. Above all, I vowed to record an indelible memory of this place because I would never, ever return. For as much positivity as it gave me, I never want to experience that degree of desperation again.

We said goodbye to one of my two closest friends that night. As with anyone departing our temporary home, he chose the food we would order for delivery and which movie we'd watch that night. For dinner, he chose for us to go to the cafeteria. It was in line with his practical nature, but I like to think he wanted to enjoy one last dinner of conversation and laughs where we'd had so many before. We watched *Planes, Trains and Automobiles*, which was an absolutely perfect representation of his humor and temperament. I've seen that movie dozens of times but it seemed completely fresh watching it with my new friends. We had made more than a few "those aren't pillows" jokes over the previous several weeks.

Journal entry: Thursday, May 19, 2022

The end is drawing near

The emotions remain so mixed

Excited. Sad.

Why does it feel the same way I did in Atlanta before I got here?

How can I replicate this?

The sleep, the structure, the people, the care

Feels so odd to be leaving

So many lasts

So many goodbyes already

This is hard

I'm proud of myself for embracing the moment

I'm proud of myself for so much

Two days before I left, it became clear what kind of shock awaited me. I had lived squarely in a green zone for more than five weeks. I would lose my cover in forty-eight hours. We were encouraged to make safety plans—and by encouraged, I mean mandated to do so, which made me somewhat prepared. I had identified doctors for direct care, made arrangements for friends and family to accompany me during the reentry, and made a list of all the changes I would need to make to my home and routine. Lists and plans are easy to write, but the reality of what lay ahead was overwhelming.

You know when you find a bunch of chemicals and cleaning agents under the sink and mix them together to see what happens? My insides felt something like that. (That may or may not be based on something my friends and I regularly did as youngsters.) Since each chemical or cleaning agent was potent on its own, I was terrified and delighted by the idea of a combination that would create a deadly and awesome explosion—so I tried them all. Anticipation, happiness, longing, fear, and grief did not ignite so much as create a noxious gas that affected my mood in the final hours.

Pride was the emotion that ruled above others on that day. I had accomplished so much in my time inside. I made an actual pen-and-paper list of achievements, ranging from coping skills to basketball prowess to completing hard conversations. I was excited to show off the fruits of my hard work to the world.

Journal entry: Friday, May 20, 2022

Reclaiming a date

This is my rebirth

Can't think of a better way to end

Great basketball (18 of 46 threes to end)

Great group sessions. Fun lunch

Goodbye ceremony. Wow. I allowed the praise

I'm smart. I'm funny. I'm a leader. I'm kind. I'm insightful

My stomach was in knots

The circle is complete

Feels like Atlanta the night before I left for here. Nervous. Unknown.

I'm not scared. I'm not so, so sad. I'm ready

This is new. Not allowing nostalgiafying

It's time to go. Show off me. Ready

I will miss people

I don't want my phone

Tomorrow is day zero

Let's do this

My father died on May 20, 2006. Every May 20 since then has felt heavy, though each year the intensity subsides. There have even been years when I didn't realize it was that day until halfway in. Yet even when I wasn't actively aware or memorializing, I would still have an uneasy and churning sensation in my core.

By absolute coincidence, my last day at the clinic was on May 20. I hadn't realized this until that day. I first vowed to reclaim that day and make it no longer a day of death but one of rebirth. This would be my day, my moment, and my anniversary. As I reflected over a final session of three-point shooting and elliptical mastery, that sentiment evolved. I couldn't let go of the existing historical importance of that day, nor did I want to.

For all the feelings I had about our relationship during my father's life, our relationship after his death has been positive and redemptive. As with all healing, time invariably moves the needle to the positive. The pain of his demise was sharp enough to seek help and become a better person. My stepmom Michele, his younger kids, Elizabeth, and I have come together in a way that wouldn't have been possible without his illness. As I dream of one day being a father, I think about all the parts I'd take from him and those I'd leave behind. Lately I've been telling more stories about those fun times with him in Florida, the boats and beaches and Buffett, and even the loopy and funny moments he had as he became more ill. Without question, my time in the clinic moved our relationship forward.

I absolutely dreaded my farewell ceremony, the moment when we'd go around the circle and receive final words of encouragement as we walked out the door. For all of my needs for validation, for all of those desperate and damaging things I did to feel the rush of approval, I have forever despised moments of potentially inauthentic praise. This includes, but is not limited to, toasts that go around a room, salespeople telling you how brilliant you are when they're trying to close a deal, and birthday parties that celebrate you solely for the accomplishment of not dying over a twelve-month period. As you can imagine, a campfire-esque send-off (with no fire, lest we go bananas and burn things down) falls squarely in my definition of ersatz adoration.

I decided, for once, to put that crippling insecurity behind me and let people speak their minds about my impact on our group. It was a lot like that third grade "special day" book in which people told me I was funny and weird. They provided the same general sentiment, maybe with some more adult language (not cuss words, just more sophisticated phrasing suitable for a mental hospital). Laughs, tears, pride, and humility were even more plentiful than the barbecue we ordered for my chosen delivery. We closed the night watching my selected film, *The Naked Gun*, to reflect my refined tastes and cinephile status.

That night, I said goodbye to the night staff, including my good friend and basketball-watching buddy Kevin. He and I built a bond, one of many between staff and patient that supersedes the underlying reasons for being in that place, at that time, in very different contexts. It was the first of a lot of hard goodbyes over the next twelve hours. I hit the pillow with a smile and tears. It's like when it's sunny and raining— it seems weird and like it shouldn't be happening, but a single umbrella keeps you dry and without sunburn. My umbrella was the comfort and confidence of the five and a half weeks of work I had done.

V.

Sweet Freedom

CHAPTER 21

TAKE ME HOME

While staying at the clinic, it was possible to leave campus for doctor's appointments. Three of my friends experienced this surreal and temporary excursion into the real world. I was blown away by the idea that someone could reexperience the outside and come back in with a full reminder of all freedoms and options out there. The visual in my mind was like Uncle Traveling Matt from *Fraggle Rock* when he explores the human world. It made me wonder what it would be like on the morning I left.

On the morning of May 21, I did a final load of laundry, watched the latest episode of *Barry*, and then slipped out the door of the unit while saying final, quiet goodbyes to the staff and my friends. I had already told them goodbye the night before, so the situation was similar to when you say bye to someone at the grocery store and then see them in the next aisle over and say, "Hey! Bye again."

Given that I was still property of the hospital, I was escorted out of the complex by our head patient safety associate. This dude was always a stickler. He made up rules that didn't exist. He strictly enforced the ones that did. He was gregarious and friendly but didn't let you get too close. He said goodbye, gave me a hug, and released me to the checkout process. A few signatures, a collection of my forbidden belongings, and a handoff of a copious amount of pills, and I was ready to roll.

Freshly released, ready to turn some doorknobs on my own

Unlike the last time I'd passed through that front door, I was alone on this part of the mission home. I went from that door directly into an awaiting Uber. I wondered what the driver was thinking as he picked up a dude with a suitcase from a mental hospital. I regret not taking the opportunity to make him a bit nervous by saying some strange sentences, but I have a 4.91 rating to uphold.

And so began my multi-phased reentry to the real world.

Phase I: Stimulus Overload

There is no way to explain how much I underappreciated light, motion, colors, sounds, and smells until I climbed into that Uber. Sure, I would have rather not smelled the specific aromas of that Chevy Traverse, but to have something—anything—different from the sterile nothingness of the unit was refreshing. So many little things hit me: the leather seat that wasn't medical-grade manufactured fabric, loud music on the radio accompanied by DJ voices, a person talking to me who wasn't one of the thirty or so I'd seen for six weeks. There were lights that weren't fluorescent. Everything was new and fresh.

Atlanta and the arms of my family were my first post-ward destinations in an effort to slow-roll back into society. I arrived at the departing airport and walked through doors that opened on their own. No locks, no keys, no alarms; just a breezy and unrestricted stroll. I slipped into autopilot based on muscle memory from hundreds of journeys through the airport gauntlet, while my head swiveled to take in all the people, foods, and shiny objects that I had been without. It was the first time in six weeks that I had been on my own for more than fifteen minutes. The air conditioning was broken in the terminal, so I sweated my way through the boarding process until I was stuffed into the window seat. It was odd—in the past, I would have been cripplingly self-conscious about my prodigious perspiration, but now I didn't care because I was too mentally distracted by all the stimuli, and I had gained the clarity that nobody noticed or cared.

Emotion overcame me as the plane took off. The last time I'd been on a runway was when I had arrived, hours away from being locked in a facility with strangers and an unknown life. Now I was flying away free, heading back to loving arms and the comforts of life. I wept. I was so excited and scared. I feared being alone again. I feared relapse. I feared that I wouldn't be accepted. Most of all, I missed my friends and my secure comfort zone.

My phone sat in my pocket, largely ignored from being out of sight and out of mind for so long. The idea of catching up on social media was daunting (it proved to be extremely easy to catch up, as nothing of importance had happened). I was happily unhitched from the tether of texting. I had limited interest in changing the phone from airplane mode because I wanted to stay underground and off the radar for as long as possible. There is so much liberty in invisibility.

Elizabeth picked me up from the Atlanta airport. She was the last family I saw on the way in and the first family I saw on the way out.

The symmetry of the experience created comfort, a metaphorical giant inflatable cushion.

I loved the home-cooked food. I loved the hugs from my mother, my brother-in-law, my nephews, and my niece. I enjoyed the candid questions from the kids. I reveled in turning doorknobs. I thoroughly enjoyed showering with water that originated from above my head. I felt warmth and safety from the memories I made on the unit. I felt confidence that I was ready for life. I squished into a lovely, soft mattress and closed my eyes for an uninterrupted sleep. Though every fifteen minutes, I felt like something was missing.

I had no idea when my RAM would run out from running too many programs and freeze my internal CPU. I knew it was inevitable.

Phase II: Harsh Return to Reality

Journal entry: Sunday, May 22, 2022

THE SECURITY IS GONE

All alone. Hard to hold on. The tears.

No sleep. Unsafe. No people. So sad.

Life goes on in the unit. No me. No status

Lost some temporary identity

Remember mindfulness. Be mindful. Be mindful. Be mindful

Heart. Chest. Pain. Memories. Blank slate

What now. Who now. Where now

Blank slate. Scary, sad, exciting

After a few days of stimulus absorption and safety monitoring in Atlanta, it was time to return to my home in Tampa. I received and deflected a flood of advice to stay with family for weeks. I didn't want to further delay what I knew would not be a fully pleasant reentry to my world.

My sister had babysat (read: extensively driven) my car, a noisy and fast beast that looks like a regular dad-mobile. It remained a time capsule of my meltdown era. There was evidence of my trips to watch UNC play in the tournament. A parking slip from a night I'd rather forget. A gaggle of empty Diet Mountain Dew bottles on the backseat floor. Even when you're spiraling toward commitment to a psych ward, one must Do the Dew.

My seven-hour drive allowed for some catching up on podcasts and a few Dairy Queen stops. It also gave me over four hundred minutes to think about all of the conversations that awaited me when I returned.

On the professional front, I was dreading a conversation with a person I respected greatly, where I would have to inform him I was declining the chief operating officer job. It was a no-brainer that I could not be successful in this job in a state of recovery. I manned up and told the executive the truth, and he could not have been more understanding. It was the first test of how I would communicate my journey in the professional world, and it gave me a lot of hope.

I also thought of all of the friends, places, and activities I would have to leave behind. The plans for my future that I had drafted on the unit included several goodbyes to parts of my old life. It's easy to think about turning down invitations, drinks, and temptations when you're sitting inside high walls in stringless athleisure for weeks on end. I was tense and anxious about looming opportunities that might sabotage or trash my plans. Thankfully I had the tools and techniques to manage the worry that I was borrowing from the future.

I pulled into my driveway early on a Wednesday evening. I was thankful that I made an effort to cleanse my house of breakdown relics before I left. No full trash cans or sink full of wine glasses. It was clean. But it smelled like I remembered, except even more potent. It was much bigger than it used to feel. It was brutally quiet, dim, and empty. It would be the site of several soul-crushing interactions and internal struggles in the ensuing days and weeks. I realized it needed an Extreme Makeover: Recovering Psych Patient Edition to transform it from old Michael's house to where new Michael could thrive. I wondered if it was even possible to pull off.

Phase III: Re-Create the Inside

I exhibited some odd behaviors in my first week back home. Although I finally had a full closet of sartorial options, I instead continued to wear a narrow and hygiene-challenged wardrobe. I forgot to eat several meals because there was no schedule or holler across the room to line up for the walk to the cafeteria. I lost a lot of weight from forgoing sustenance, returning to an active life in which I regularly walked more than twenty feet, and continuing to avoid alcohol. I also found myself experiencing FOMO about what was happening back on the unit. I started really missing the people, the process, and the structure, so I took steps to re-create the experience at home.

At first, it was hard to muster the courage to be around other people, considering that I lived alone and was isolating myself from the shame of the imaginary judgment radiating from my neighbors. The last time they had seen me, I was a drunk mess. For six weeks, they knew I was "away somewhere without my phone." I figured that they'd heard about my confessed transgressions since I came home, though logic would state otherwise. My default was to be unhealthily alone all the time.

So I took action to surround myself with other humans, even if I didn't know any of them. Instead of at-home workouts, I ventured into the gym. Rather than write at home, I went to the nearby bustling food hall (one of those fancy food courts in an old sock factory or whatever trendy redevelopment project happens in the cool parts of cities). I made a point to go to in-person church rather than watching online. The point is that whenever it was an option, I tried to err on the side of being near others. Eventually, I opened myself up to social experiences, even hockey games. Those games were rather overwhelming, not only for the large crowd but also the odd rules.

Next, I rebuilt an infrastructure of care that continued the work I did on the psych ward. I started an intensive outpatient program at a nearby psychiatric facility. It gave me another set of peers and professionals to help me regain footing in a new life. Three days a week, from nine in the morning until early afternoon, I experienced what looked like a similar schedule to what I had while I was an inpatient.

But within three weeks, I'd had enough. The returns diminished. The all-encompassing intensity of my inpatient time could not be replicated. The people, the structure, and the facility outshined every element of the Tampa program. I just couldn't duplicate the experience, and I didn't want to. I wanted to keep the memories and lessons of my time on the unit as indelible and detailed as possible.

I found, instead, that setting up a cadence of therapist sessions, psychiatrist visits, and church groups was the best option for me. I have been lucky to find an outstanding set of men and women to act as a care team on the outside. These weekly appointments and meetings provided the basis for a structured schedule, which I developed to mirror the rigor and order that I had experienced while inside the clinic.

I had found a groove. I felt confident that a new set of guardrails were in place and I had built a foundation to start layering in more elements of a complete life.

Phase IV: Bad Idea Jeans

Irrational confidence typically comes from a lack of challenge, a void of healthy guidance from trusted peers, and underestimation of the adversary. Just like when I was on that Mississippi River cruise where I practiced shuffleboard for three days, thought I was awesome, and then lost fifty to zero against eighty-year-old women. Irrational confidence grows with boredom and isolation. Clearly, I was in a position to get owned based on my own terrible judgment in my abilities.

Case in point: I once thought it would be a great idea to test my two-week-old new way of living, stability, and sobriety by going to someone's twenty-first birthday party in Las Vegas.

Let's be clear—this was a family birthday party. We were celebrating my niece, who is actually the daughter of my close friend/big brother from my consulting days and who I consider family. The group was half college kids and half adults (i.e., people who had jobs). I had built protections for myself by flying in Saturday afternoon and leaving first thing Sunday morning (thus avoiding the carnage of the day club, which I recommend to nobody above the age of twenty-one years and one day). I told a few of the adults to look out for me and talk sense into me if I looked like I was going to be a moron. I felt safe and confident.

I've been to Vegas roughly fifty times in my life, starting when I was fifteen years old. It has been a special place for me for decades. My mom and I used to go every summer when I was in high school. I wrote my AP American History term paper about the development and growth of Las Vegas (I got a good grade, in spite of Mr. Plyler wondering what in the world I was going to write about). As I grew into adulthood, the city transitioned to become my prime spot for romantic getaways, sporting events, and general debauchery. I've won money, lost my dignity, and made friends. Of course, it also devolved into a terrifying black hole as my alcohol abuse got worse, but I tend to forget that (because I never remembered it in the first place).

Now, it wasn't the noise, the racy billboards, or the alcohol that attacked me from the moment I stepped foot in McCarran Airport. It was the memories that came back in 4K high-definition detail and tried to take me down. For the next twelve hours, I traversed casinos, restaurants, and even dirty staircases on crosswalks that stabbed me with microscopic flashbacks from nearly thirty years of mental recordings. I took repeated punches to the chest through happy hour, dinner, and blackjack (which I was no longer able to ease with a steady buffet of double Jack and Diets). I felt the ghost of a former girlfriend who is now long gone from my life, one with whom I'd had a wonderful weekend a few years back. Memories and mistakes poured over me like champagne at the terrible club in which I once embarrassed myself during my consulting days. I suffered through every nail in my skin until I threw in the towel at 11:00 p.m., executing a fine Irish Exit to "go to the bathroom." I didn't see the group again.

A sleepless night at the Aria bled into a drowsy return to the airport and a flight to Tampa via Dallas-Fort Worth. During the layover, I plopped onto a stool at a Cowboys-themed restaurant for a salad and a deep breath. In a poetically absurd, one-in-a-million happenstance, I looked to my right, and there sat one of the many women I had angered over the years. Needless to say, she gave me an icy, shocked reception. In the past, I would have turned on some false charm, acted happy to see her, and survived the situation with no further damage. At that moment, I was broken. I told her everything that happened over the last several months. I didn't apologize. I didn't pander. I didn't patronize. I just sat there, mumbled, and drank my Diet Coke while staring at the floor. She later told me she didn't recognize that person. I didn't know if that was good or bad. I still don't.

Phase V: Send Me Back In

Journal entry: Tuesday, July 5, 2022

Yesterday was the Fourth of July. I knew it would be a tough day. There are people who were once in my life that no longer are. There are fun places to which I am no longer invited. There are countless beers left in the cooler because I'm not drinking them anymore. I miss all of those things to the point of agony. They are not coming back. I accept that.

Predictably, yesterday was awful. I am emotionally sore. I can feel the same pangs, the same creeping thoughts that seeded my meltdown in the spring.

I woke up on July 5 with a false hangover. One of the oddest parts of ending alcohol abuse is that your body still relies on a conditioned timer to think it is a wreck after a weekend of consecutive drinking. Headaches, shakes, thirst—all of it would come to me for the first twelve seconds after waking up until I remembered I'd had nothing to drink. Part of me felt proud and relieved. The rest of me felt sad I had done nothing social or exciting enough to merit a legit withdrawal.

The excitement and intrigue of returning home after a semi-incarcerated kind of life had completely given way to the reality that I was alone, jobless, companionless, and overall lost in a world that looked the same but felt like Mars. I had nothing on my calendar that day and could not motivate myself to do anything resembling productivity. Most adult and able-bodied Americans were at work. I was a shame burrito shuffling around my house, an athleisure tortilla containing a filling of misery and regret. There was absolutely nothing to distract or push me to do more than live in my own self-pity.

I learned in the clinic that when I start to feel myself sliding into depression, I should do the opposite of the negative behavior I was compelled to do. In this case, that meant removing my aluminum foil wrap of sadness to leave the house and immerse myself in the world. This is easier said than done when you have no reasonable place to go. I got in the car without a destination. I drove aimlessly through South Tampa, scrolling through all the options of places with open doors, people, and no expectation to engage with anyone.

My first thought was church. That's where people in the movies go when they need to be contemplative and found sitting alone by a precocious ne'er-do-well for a heartwarming moment like the shovel man in *Home Alone*. So off I went to my church, where I found a locked door because it was a Tuesday and it wasn't Christmas Eve in the north suburbs of Chicago.

In what would become the saddest realization in my post-clinic life to date, the only other place I could think of was Walmart. Perhaps because of its proximity; perhaps because if you need anything at all—paint, Bugles, or psychological Robitussin—you can find it at Walmart. I recommend you never aspire to go to a Walmart solely because you have nowhere else to go. It does have some satisfying elements, like people-watching and camouflage product bingo, but I can confirm that it does not offer a long-term solution.

I roamed around the store for twenty minutes or so, teary-eyed with the existential desperation of seeking salvation at a big-box discounter.

All I could think at that moment was how much I missed the order and comfort of the unit. There was a social structure. There was a soft-serve machine. For every minute of the day, there was a purpose. For every day of the week, there was a goal. For every week of the month, there was a noticeable and positive change in my life. I wanted to go back. I missed my friends. The outside life wasn't for me. It made me finally understand Brooks Hatlen from *The Shawshank Redemption*.

I called some of my friends from the program. They were going through the same thing. We felt defeated by the real world and just wanted our little community back. This continued for weeks. Eventually, as life became fuller, the feeling waned. Freedom, unlocked door-knobs, and shoelaces are a good thing. But still, to this day, I have the occasional desire to want to hop the fence the other way.

Phase VI: Defiance

Journal entry: Tuesday, July 5, 2022 (continued)

My job now is to put everything I learned to use. I'm doing it. And I don't quit. I keep pounding. I remember to talk to myself as I would to a friend. This too shall pass. There is happiness ahead. You have no idea what God has in store. You have lost a lot, but you will gain more than you could have imagined. You don't know why this is happening but you know it's not for nothing. You stay patient. You are a good person who made some mistakes. Things happened to you that weren't your fault. You were brave to get help when you did. It could have been much worse if you hadn't gotten help.

Now it's time to go back out with your head high and to refocus on what is productive. Get your writing done. Keep playing ball. Own your story and don't let others define you. Now get back out there.

Bruce sings in "Dancing in the Dark" that he wants to change everything about himself—his home, his clothes, his hair, and even his face.

That sentiment kicked in for me as I bounced off of the nadir of my post-clinic experience. I decided that neither my depression, my irrational musings to go back, nor the ghost of old me would claim victory. I would instead retrench, tar my heels, and show the intangible-but-very-real enemy who was boss.

I needed to change myself and my environment. I considered selling my house and moving closer to family, though somehow that felt like a defeat. Instead, I moved furniture and wall hangings, added lights to my backyard, and rid myself of all major belongings that reminded me of people who were no longer in my life. I was Peter Venkman roaming my house with a Ghostbusters proton pack (trash bag), exorcizing as much as I could that reminded me of the old life I'd left behind.

I felt extremely compelled (and still do) to "change my clothes, my hair, my face." I got to work in my closet throwing out old shirts that didn't fit, ones that I had kept for years with the expectation that I'd return to my early-thirties, running-thirty-miles-a-week physique. I threw out anything given to me by an old flame. The most effective, symbolic, and literal move was to trash all the shoes I wore while living my worst life. No shoe—athletic, dress, or casual—would get a free pass. I didn't want to walk in the shoes of a dude who hated me so much (the feeling was mutual).

As for my hair, that one's pretty simple. I haven't cut it since I left for the psych ward. For context, I used to get a haircut about every three weeks with a "high and tight" instruction for the barber. Two faded to one on the sides; keep the top short. Now my head is really hot. I use a blow dryer, and I've got some solid wings on the side and wake at the back. I have to cut it sometime, as it's threatening to become the Phil-Collins-at-Wembley-'87 look. My hairline is hanging on for dear life through Rogaine and prayers, but it's getting slipperier up there.

My face shrank ever since I stopped drinking and worked out more. Thus, I changed my face. The "Dancing in the Dark" transformation challenge was complete. I added another, perhaps more modern (and shocking to those who know me) touch-up in the form of my first-ever tattoos. I have always been rather anti-tattoo, not out of principle or fashion but because I can't think of anything so permanent in my life that I would want an indelible bumper sticker promoting it. Halfway through my time inside the clinic, I did a one-eighty.

As the weeks progressed inside, I collected several bracelets and accoutrement to remind me to take things a day at a time, to be who I am, and to retain and build on the progress I was making. I knew it would be cumbersome and kind of weird to wear a bunch of bracelets in the real world, so I decided to replace them with two small tattoos at the base of my thumbs. I would be able to see them, but most others wouldn't notice.

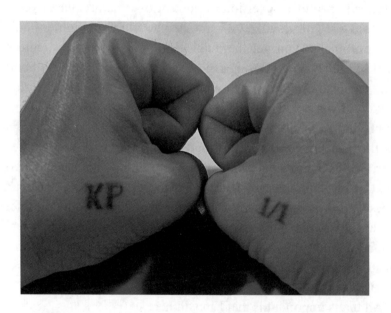

On the left hand: *Keep pounding*. Technically, yes, it's the Carolina Panthers mantra. It's also a reminder to me that I am strong enough to handle obstacles—even the invisible and irrational ones.

On the right hand: *One decision at a time, one day at a time*. Even if I've made ten straight questionable decisions, there's always an opportunity to take the best course available at the next crossroad.

Phase VII: Stasis

My grandfather Archie loved to build fires. Since I wanted to do every-thing that he did, I followed his every move to learn the ways of a per-fect inferno. I got a little too interested in it, to the point of pyromania (sorry Morrocroft Neighborhood Association for the permanent scar in the neighborhood park).

I've always been fascinated by the various states of energy con-sumption and disbursement from a fire. In the beginning, it's a calm pile of wood. Then a number of exogenous interjections (a match, some rolls of the Shelby Star, maybe a little or a whole lot of lighter fluid) creates a flurry of flame and heat that is exciting and dangerous, a strangely primitive exertion of control over nature. Then you have to prod it a few times to get it right, maybe add more lighter fluid, and then, eventually, you get the magical glow and hum of a controlled fire. The little snaps, whooshes of gas releases, and crackles of burning wood always mesmerized me while my clothes absorbed the glorious stink of a natural fire.

I feel like I've been that fire over the last several weeks. After flame-ups, flameouts, and a few sparks that spat toward those who hovered too close, I'm in a nice steady burn. I know what my challenges are. I am proud of my progress, and I'm ready to slowly approach what's next. I miss the clinic, but I don't want to go back. I keep up with a few of my people from the unit, but not everyone. I'm talking to people about jobs, but I'm not committing to anything yet. I'm bruised, I'm sore, and sometimes I'm sad. But I'm ready with a set of tools and processes to take on what's next.

All that's important is that I'm still here.

CHAPTER 22

LEARNING TO FLY

When you're a management consultant, you are told you must have structure to your answers, whether it's in a case interview to get the job or when you're in front of a client. A good structure usually has three components. People can remember things in threes. Well, I'm here to tell you good structure isn't always that clean, and I'm about to blow your mind and hit you with groups of four.

It took several weeks to distill a month and a half of psychiatric, psychological, and social learnings into a manageable buffet of resources that I can lean on when things get rough. There are salads of boring-but-long-term beneficial sustenance. There are protein-rich prime filets of confidence that build strong bones to withstand everyday life's body shots. There are side dishes that I bring in to accompany the entrées when I'm facing particular flavors of hardship. And, of course, there are the desserts—injections of joy that may not lead to anything physically beneficial, but sure do feel good.

At this point, I will remind you that I am not a doctor. I am not a professional, and I am not you. I simply want to impart what I have learned in case there are useful tools here that you can bring into your own life. Once again, I would like to reiterate that this book has made countless references to trash reality television and should not be seen as any source of professional guidance.

With that said, there are eight primary lessons that I have taken with me; each has specific tactical implications and actions that I have adopted. These eight divide equally into groups of four (I am raging against the consulting machine; I trust you can handle it) across two categories: Intrinsic and Perpetual, and Practical and Concrete.

Category	Learning
Intrinsic and Perpetual	1. Treat anxiety and depression like a wound
	2. Thrive on self-generated validation
	3. Stare down and defeat shame
	4. Steer the car on the road you're driving
Practical and Concrete	5. Untether from addictions
	6. Quiet the digital noise
	7. Carry a daily scorecard
	8. Seek the life-giving

- Intrinsic and Perpetual: These are the insights and goal posts that I can't measure or "check off." Instead, they are constant battles against my own insecurities and conditions. They are ever-present, require a reliable internal meter, and will always be a challenge.

- Practical and Concrete: These goal posts are more easily grasp-able. They generally have "yes/no" answers for "did I do these today?" and have the benefit of being reset at any moment. I can declare that yesterday was a loss but today will be a win—or maybe even decide that for the rest of the day I'll do better.

Most of these lessons seem very squishy or unrealistic. They evoke inspirational posters featuring cats or *American Idol* medleys against a backdrop of a children's choir. I get that, but I am living by these and have very tactical steps that I take to live them. They're not just bumper stickers affixed to a Prius.

Intrinsic and Perpetual Learnings

1. Treat Anxiety and Depression Like a Wound

- Think of them as conditions and symptoms that indicate deeper whys.
- Give them attention and remember they aren't weaknesses.
- Gauge their validity and magnitude by asking challenging questions.

Let's say, in a totally hypothetical and definitely-not-drawn-from-life event, you were to find yourself wounded in multiple places on your body. There's blood rolling down your leg, a gash on your arm, and a strange coating of orange rust on your clothing and limbs. It's an all-around bad scene. You go to the emergency room, and they ask what's happening. Would you tell them that you're suffering from bleeding? Technically, yes, it's true. However, the doctor would likely expect the thirty-one-year-old man standing in front of her to explain the underlying incident that created the carnage. That it was an intense Rollerblading accident involving a hill, a baby stroller, and a bridge at White Rock Lake in Dallas would be important to know. In this particular case, I think it would be understandable that the person in question would offer a cooler and tougher version of the injury story that left out being a grown man on Rollerblades.

I've learned to manage depression and anxiety similarly and without Rollerblades. I used to lament how I was depressed or full of anxiety but never questioned what was creating them. My body was telling me that something was wrong, either temporary or chronic, and that I needed to make a change or address the issue directly. I lingered far too long in relationships, jobs, and housing situations, to name only a few conditions. I would retrench and push further against the pain. This repression is what we learned in our sports practices and social training as boys and men in the south. So like Willis Reed saving the Knicks, Kerri Strug winning the gold, or Lisa Turtle dancing "The Sprain" to win the contest at The Max, we fight through the pain to avoid showing weakness. Please take it from me that this can lead to a visit to a mental hospital.

I can't speak for every individual medical situation, though I can tell you that medication has been helpful in managing the physical pain and mental distortion that anxiety and depression spark. As of now, I take two medications that work with each other to smooth my crags and canyons into rolling hills. I have also learned how to administer equally, if not more, effective doses of critical self-questioning to combat my conditions. When mired in the deepest valleys of despair or impaled by the sharpest stakes of anxiety, I stop and ask myself a few important questions: Are these feelings supported by facts? Does the reality on the ground merit this sharp of a reaction? Am I just sad about Barbara Hershey dying at the end of *Beaches*?

Once I have a tighter grip on the matter at hand, I'm able to work toward soothing myself via a number of available therapies and levers. Sometimes I write. Sometimes I exercise. Sometimes I run. Sometimes I hide from the world. No matter what, I never ignore what I'm feeling, and I do not intend to fall back on any of the short-term injections that eased my pains in the past.

2. Thrive on Self-Generated Validation

- Strip away the distractions to understand true identity and motivations.
- Attribute a sense of accomplishment to only authentic metrics.
- Pay attention to the happy feelings, and do more of what led to them.

Yesterday, while driving from Atlanta to Tampa, I caught up with a colleague from my consulting days. He and I worked very closely together from the first day I showed up as an intern. He was my first project manager, an advocate for me to become partner, and a frequent recipient of my venting about career stress and panic modes. We spent the first twenty minutes or so discussing the goings-on of the firm (where he still works). We discussed the trajectory of the firm's revenue, his recent promotion and high-status title, and the headline news involving new partner promotions and the restructuring of the firm's geographic footprint. I found it fascinating, informative, and as relatable to me as interstellar exploration.

I understood all the words and concepts but could not believe that it was a description of a company for which I spent ten years toiling. This is not an indictment—it is only to say that knowing what I know now, it's unfathomable that I had thrived. I was never cut out for that job, but the promise of status, money, and the solid gold of external, objective validation had driven me to permanent residency outside my mental safety zone. I had ridden that barrel of misguided ambition over a waterfall of chaos and landed right in a corporate pond, where I was forced to lay off scores of people and fight against gale-force organizational headwinds. Although looking back, it was more like that Weather Channel guy who didn't have to do all that fighting against a light wind. He just wanted it to seem dramatic and difficult.

I have never been motivated by money or titles. I know that. And yet, I chased them. Being isolated from outside distractions reminded me that I thrive on helping people, making people smile, and creating something new. If I can do those three things in a given day, it's been a good day. As I reenter the professional world, I've never been more confident that I will find the right career in which I will provide real value to people and be happy. Said another way, I have self-generated validation for the first time in my life.

Of course, it's easy for a person with resources to drop everything, write a book that nobody asked for, and say "follow your heart!" But it's possible to find self-validation in any facet of life, as long as you understand what really motivates you and makes you feel accomplished. It might be growing a new plant in the garden or finding a cause for which to volunteer. Whatever it is, trust that positive feeling you have when you go to bed at night, and then do more of what created it.

3. Stare Down and Defeat Shame

- Nobody talks or thinks about you as much as you think they do; you're not that interesting.
- Manage and reduce shame by talking about it with trusted confidants.
- Mirror self-speak with language used toward friends and loved ones.

The flow of a client meeting in management consulting is pretty consistent. The three or four most senior members of the consulting team sit in a room with five or six of the most senior client executives. Everyone sits (according to a carefully orchestrated seating plan) around what is usually a sterile boardroom table. Each place setting has a couple of trees' worth of printed PowerPoint materials and a bottle of water. The senior partner kicks off the meeting with a short preamble/pledge of allegiance to the client. The senior project manager then takes the reins and walks the client through a wildly complex set of data and unrealistic recommendations. Every now and then, said project manager tosses the proverbial microphone over to a more junior staffer to explain a ridiculously dense vein of insights and beautiful graphs.

I equally desired and dreaded these opportunities to shine. In the right settings, you feel like Snoop Dogg adding an impeccable guest verse to a song. But in the wrong context and without the right transition, it feels more like you're John Mayer popping onto the stage at a Taylor Swift concert. Fear, rational or irrational, of the latter situations generated tremendous anxiety for me before and during meetings. Often, I'd sweat, stammer, and stutter over whatever slide I was presenting to a dumbfounded crowd of businesspeople and nerds. I would then punish myself for days about how bad I had botched my guest appearance. I would assume that the clients were making fun of me and that the partners were preparing my scathing performance review.

Over time, I changed my mental narrative. I built the confidence that nobody in the room knew this information better than I did. I trusted that

I had practiced as much as I could in the mirror and knew that I was as prepared as possible. Finally, I remembered that it was highly unlikely that anybody in the room was really paying that much attention to me. They were thinking about the calls and emails they were missing, the tasks that remained ahead of them before they could go home, and why we didn't order lunch for a noon meeting. I would then debrief with the clients and partners to go over any open issues or questions that came from the meeting and assess whether I'd handled the situation effectively.

I realize now that the feeling I was combatting was essentially professional shame. Personal shame is a demon I will never stop fighting. I have executed more infractions against people I care about and against myself than I care to number. I have spent years drinking to the point of blackout with no idea what I said or did. I have broken trust. I have broken promises. I have lied. I have done all of these things in both small and large measures and punished myself to the fullest extent of the self-defined law. Ultimately, it was shame that inspired the thought of literally crashing my life to a halt on that interstate in North Carolina. Shame is the feeling that I fear the most, and it has the most potential to create relapses and further damage.

My time in the psych ward taught me ways to ease the impact of shame. I'm now able to bring foamy jets of logic into the blazing dumpster fire that shame creates. I cannot emphasize enough to myself that people are just not thinking or talking about me as much as I think they are. We are not that interesting to other people; it is both a sad and a comforting fact. Salacious information tends to spread quickly and get people talking. The perception that this is happening about me has led to multiple bouts of horror. It still can, especially when I think that all of South Tampa is talking about the guy who went to a loony bin. Only now, I can think clearly enough to know that nobody really cares after they hear something the first time.

Of course, "I'm not as interesting as I think I am" thoughts do not help incidents of shame related to badly hurting people that you love. I have deep gashes on my conscience related to what I've done to a few specific people in my most broken moments. I can't go back in time and change what I did, but I can talk to trusted people to gauge how much I should be punishing myself. I had invaluable moments of truth and vulnerability in telling my stories to trusted colleagues on the unit. Hearing confirmation of "Yep, that is bad," followed by "You're not the first one to do that kind of thing" initiated a process of self-forgiveness. Bringing a shame-generating moment into the open is like hydrogen peroxide on a wound. Satisfying bubbles of empathy from trusted confidants is a first step to cleansing.

I've also found immense value in talking to myself in the same way I would talk to a friend. During one group therapy session at the clinic, I spoke of what I considered to be a particularly horrific incident about which I harbor superyachts of shame. The doctor leading the group asked me to roleplay how I would talk to my best friend if they came to me with the same situation. I said, "This is a tough situation, but I am here for you. I understand you feel shame, but know that this could have happened to a lot of people. So far, you've made the best decisions and taken the most honorable actions you can. Lots of people, including me, still love you and will stand by you. Your true friends will support you, and you're not a bad person." It was a very different tone and set of words than what I was telling myself.

Once I learned to be as supportive, reassuring, and empathetic to myself as I am to other people, the shame monster was tamed, chained, and sent to the basement. He may still grunt and rattle the chains, but he's under control.

4. Steer the Car on the Road You're Driving

- Live in the present; it's the only option.
- Control the controllable (self-reactions), and let go of the uncontrollable (others' reactions).
- Actively seek and utilize mindfulness techniques to stay in the present.

When I was little, I was driving a golf cart at my grandparents' friends' house. It was a huge lakefront estate on a hill in the far reaches of civilization. It was awesome. As a ten-year-old, to drive a golf cart was to be a king, a NASCAR Winston Cup champion—to be *the* King Richard Petty. At roughly eleven miles per hour, I explored the grounds along with a dumb, happy golden retriever riding shotgun.

The land had a few challenging components, namely a system of retaining walls that managed the grade of the steep terrain from house to dock. I all but ignored these while zooming and cornering about the acreage until a near disaster that dropped the red flag on my traverse. I was in a pedal-to-the-medal reverse maneuver when I heard a shout and noticed that I was speeding toward the edge of a terrace, about to spill backward over one of the retaining walls. I slammed on the brakes just in time. The tires hugged the edge of the retaining wall. My heart was pounding somewhere in my throat. Luckily, the dog was not smart enough to know what was happening. The nearby adults laughed in relief while a combination of gratitude and embarrassment washed over me.

All I could think was how close a call it was. I quickly went through all the scenarios of falling over the wall—long-term paralysis, destroyed property, a cloud of dog fur. The anxiety of the moment took over. I was unable to shake the horror. I gathered myself, took a few deep breaths, and pressed on. And by "pressed on," I mean pressed hard on the gas without remembering to put the cart back into forward gear. Off I tumbled, backward over the wall, dog and all.

Somehow the golf cart, the dog, and I all came out relatively unscathed. In fact, the dog didn't budge. He didn't even evacuate the cart when it came to rest. He was in the moment and ready for whatever was next. I, on the other hand, had been so stuck in replaying what had happened moments before the crash that I wasn't mindful of the need to make changes to navigate myself out of the mess that I was in. Such has been the case for most of my life—focusing more on what happened before and what may or may not happen next and not paying enough attention to what's happening presently.

I have learned exactly how much of my emotional torment comes from living in the past and future. It comes out to roughly 99 percent. There are only rare moments when there is something directly in my path that I need to negotiate—other than that, I'm replaying how badly I botched that one part of my speech in seventh grade or fretting what a future reader of this book will think about me when they realize how much the seventh-grade speech contest still haunts me. Living in the moment is our only viable option; otherwise, we are wasting emotional time and energy. Short of having on hand a mad scientist, a stainless steel quasi-sports car, and 1.21 gigawatts, we aren't able to replay the past. And even if we could, it may turn into a really questionable Ashton Kutcher movie about the butterfly effect.

On top of spending time litigating the past and predicting the future, I have often found myself trying to control how other people react to stimuli that I experience or put into the world. This generates pointless mind-racing because we can't control how other people react to situations, only how we react to them. We can be ready and prepared for circumstances that may arrive, as complex as they may be. Jeff Goldblum anticipated what the enemies would do, so he stayed cool as a cucumber while he connected to an alien spacecraft's Wi-Fi signal and uploaded a file that was compatible with an operating system developed on another planet. He didn't know exactly what was going to happen, but he was prepared. We can only drive our own car (or spacecraft) and do our part to not create a wreck.

Inside the unit, my peers and I learned several methods to make sure we are living in the moment versus spinning on other temporal planes. My favorite one that I still use almost every day is to count objects in the room. I dart my eyes across the walls, the floor, the ceiling, and the space in between and count the things I see. It gives me something to do to stop my brain from spinning. It reminds me that I'm sitting right there, right then; I'm alive, and I'm present. Sometimes I recite the alphabet backward. Sometimes I do a full, guided meditation that I find online. I highly encourage everyone to study these techniques. There are countless examples out there, and they really work.

Practical and Concrete Learnings

5. Untether from Addictions and Compulsions

- Be honest about chemical addictions and identify underlying drivers.

- Inventory, name, and check all addictions and compulsions, even if they're not "traditional."

- Make concrete plans and rules to reinforce positive behaviors and avoid negative outcomes.

It's well documented throughout this book that I drank too much, too frequently, and too loosely. When I was inside the clinic, I attended numerous groups, seminars, and therapy sessions regarding alcohol addiction and abuse. It's a hard thing to admit that you've lost control of yourself when it comes to any chemical substance. But I learned that there's no shame in getting help and that each day after you admit it is another day you can live in freedom.

I am not physically addicted to alcohol. I can be around it, and I can even taste it without feeling an urge or need to drink to excess. I do know that it's an addiction insomuch as I must drink when I am in the depths of shame, guilt, and general chaos. That trio visited me regularly while I was in my descent toward breakdown. I have to keep them away if I am to stay away from my old, terrible friend: alcohol.

My real addiction is to validation. It releases endorphins that give me a rush. It can come in the form of a social media "like" or a compliment from a stranger. It can be a knowing and admiring glance at my car. It can be a laugh at a joke that I make. This is the addiction that underpinned all of my issues with alcohol and the damage booze caused to my career and social life.

I'm also burdened with a handful of compulsions. The fitness tracker on my Apple Watch owned me to the point that I would be in a bad mood if I didn't close my rings. I would remove myself from social situations to get my last few active minutes on the record. I have a compulsion to rewatch the same television shows and movies ad nauseam. I could go on, but I'm sure you get the point.

I've made a plan to overcome these addictions, and it's an every-day battle. I have entered a twelve-step program to give my addic-tions to God and move on from them. It's hard, especially since it's not a "traditional" addiction. It's mine; I own it, and it underpins my surface-level issues. To help with tactical management, I have hard and fast rules around alcohol consumption. I've stopped wearing my Apple Watch. I've watched dozens of movies and TV shows that I have missed in all of *The Office* reruns. It turns out that *Breaking Bad* is pretty good.

I do anything I can to concretely stay away from the compulsions that amplified my issues. So far, it's working. Freedom from alcohol abuse has changed my day-to-day life, my relationships, and my sense of self-worth. It has cleared the fog from my cheap sunglasses and allowed me to focus on my real psychological challenges.

6. Quiet the Digital Noise

- Ingest need-to-know information; tune out the firehose of opinion and speculation.
- Immerse in real life, and use social media for kids, dogs, and humblebragging.
- Prioritize human connection over Wi-Fi connection.

At no point during my stay did we watch cable news in the common TV room. It was a commonsense, unwritten rule employed to avoid undue strife or conflict between patients suffering from psychological crises. After a few weeks, it simply felt good not to watch. And yet we missed absolutely no important news that had a real impact on the world or ourselves as individuals. That's because hardly anything that happened over six weeks impacted us directly, and when it did, we heard about it from friends and family. I certainly do not condone being uninformed or ignorant, nor do I believe that we should ignore the challenges and horrors that face people, populations, and nations. I only wish to share the benefits and bliss of micro-dosing the news.

What we did "miss" were three networks taking singular headlines and stretching them into seventy-two hours of speculation, conjecture, and inflamed opinion. Once a day, someone would check news headlines, and if there was something interesting, we'd talk about it rationally and respectfully as a group. Instead of huddling around a crackling television spewing confirmatory or inflammatory red meat, we had deep one-on-one conversations about our lives at home and how we were feeling. I know the seventeen people I intersected with on the unit better than almost any adult I have met in the last ten years because we connected in real life, not on social media or politics. To this day, I have no idea about the politics or voting records of the friends I met there. We were all far better for it.

After six weeks without social media, I speculated that I would experience a massive rush of important life moments and milestones that I had missed while on lockdown. Spoiler alert: I only missed a lot of bumper sticker "debates" over hot-button sociopolitical issues, legs that look like hot dogs by a pool, and four thousand last-day-of-school pictures that are apparently required in order for kids to advance to the next grade. I did miss a few marriages, new kids, and some dog content. Social media has its place, but it doesn't occupy the bandwidth that it once did for me.

Before I entered the clinic, all of these screens and sources of digital stimuli had invaded my life to the point that they stole joy. Turns out I was happiest without my phone. It's unrealistic to think I can replicate that condition at home, but I have kicked my phone and my television remote out of my bedroom after ten at night. I've never slept better.

It's a shame that it took several weeks in a psych ward to understand how the overload of information we receive every day creates undue anxiety, anger, and animosity. I could have saved many thousands of dollars by turning off the TV and ignoring social media. With the onslaught of information coming at us, maybe twelve-foot brick walls, locked doors, and constant monitoring *are* required to pull us away. I recommend that everyone set boundaries and allow your brain some room to think for yourself and talk to others for perspective.

7. Carry a Daily Scorecard

- Keep a daily schedule no matter your professional or life status.
- Develop a list of daily tasks and goals.
- Maintain momentum and keep pounding.

As of typing this sentence, I have not had a real job in over seven months. Of course, a chunk of that time was spent under tight surveillance and scheduling, but there have been two and a half months of unstructured time since I came home. In the past, that level of freedom would have allowed the gasses of unproductive self-talk and damaging behavior to creep into the unguarded crevices of my existence. That's why I keep a weekly Excel spreadsheet with a framework of how to spend each day.

There are three components to the spreadsheet. First, a wake-up-until-bedtime schedule of activities in thirty-minute chunks. Second, a checklist of the five activities that I strive to do every day. Third, a list of tasks that I create the day before and throughout the current day (including several that I add after doing them when they weren't originally on the list, to make myself seem even more productive).

Importantly, this tool is not intended to be a strict timetable with a bell and a roll call. Instead, it serves as both a means of *defense* against a bad mental health day and a means of *offense* to power through what could potentially be a challenging time. There are days when I'm lost, when I don't want to get out of the bed, and when I would prefer to watch the entire first season of *The O.C.* The schedule is an inner Luke Ward welcoming me to Orange County, shoving me into productivity, and giving me a set of goals to accomplish. When I'm at my best, I challenge myself to follow the schedule diligently and check off the longest possible list of tasks in a single day.

The most important component of the schedule has been the five consistent daily goals:

1. Spend time with God
2. Play basketball
3. Practice the guitar
4. Do a legit workout
5. Write

My rules are simple and achievable: I must do at least one of these every day. If I do two or three, I give myself grace and consider it a successful day. If I do four of them, it's a big win. All five, it's the EGOT of my personal daily achievement, and that day goes in the hall of fame.

During my decades in the wilderness, I had lost touch with any semblance of the Christian foundations instilled within me as a kid. As I was tumbling to the bottom of my breakdown, I took the first steps to rediscovering what Jesus did on the cross. When I was in the unit, I made the decision to start and end every day with God. I carried with me to the psych ward the armor of a Bible, a daily devotional book, and my own rudimentary ability to pray. As I grew closer to Jesus and the sense that my past is forgiven, I was able to wipe clean the messy Etch a Sketch of who I had become to redraw who I wanted to be. Since I've been home, I've been on a mission to read the entire Bible in one calendar year, and I have dedicated time and resources toward my home church. There aren't proper words to explain what this devotion has done for me. I prioritize my time with God over all else and rarely miss a day.

Playing basketball and practicing guitar are two activities that brought me freedom and gave me life inside the clinic. These are two joys I abandoned in my youth but that tap into core parts of my identity—music and sports. I'm absolutely terrible at both, but the improvement is enough to build my spirit. At this point, I'd say I'm in the Sam Perkins "loaf around and shoot threes" stage of my basketball career and the "special guest on stage at the Pearl Jam show playing a G chord the whole time on an unplugged amplifier" level of my axe-wielding ability.

Exercising my body and my mind has long been a staple of sustaining my spirit, all three of which (body, mind, and spirit) were lost as I was spiraling. Writing this book has given me purpose and challenged my brain to stay in shape. As I've shed the alcohol and damaging behavior of my past, I've developed clarity of thought that I haven't had since I was throttling past my peers on my second lap of sixth grade. Dropping my bad habits has also upped my cardio game. Unfortunately, my Achilles tendons and general large, old-man stature have ended my running days, but I slay it on the stationary equipment. If there's ever a World Series of Elliptical Training, look for me accepting the championship belt. As long as it's healthy and mind-clearing exercise and not an irrational compulsion, I'm here for it.

I view each day as an independent event. I have had days during which I do none of the big five goals and never make it out of the house. I leave those days behind, wake up, and keep pounding. Every day is a new opportunity to win.

8. Seek the Life-Giving

- Boldly eliminate people, places, and things that deplete emotional reservoirs.
- Actively seek people and activities that enable best-self mode.
- Grieve what's left behind; focus on the positive ahead.

I do my best to simplify my life with binary evaluations. I find it is an easier way of distilling the stimuli of the world than multidimensional matrices and metrics (thus proving that I have broken free from the surly bonds of management consulting). I have some examples for you.

- NFL quarterbacks: would I be happy with him on my team or not?
- Weather: shorts or not shorts?
- Watchability of a *Saved by the Bell* episode: with or without Tori?

Elizabeth introduced me to the most helpful filter in my life—is a person, event, behavior, way of speaking, hobby, or anything at all "life-giving" or "life-taking"? There's no singular meter to determine the answer; it's up to the individual. My scoreboard is how I feel after the fact. Am I energized or exhausted? Am I proud or ashamed? Am I "good sore" (e.g., a great workout) or "bad sore" (e.g., fell off a table)?

In the sensory and activity deprivation tank of a mental institution, there was plenty of time to reflect on which elements of my life fell into which category. I had to make a list of which components of my life I wanted to eliminate for good. Most of the decisions were relatively easy, particularly those that involved wasteful and inefficient travel, empty calories, and dreaded activities and events. Where it got hard was people.

Culling people from your life is a necessary and heartbreaking part of renewal. I've made several cuts, sometimes telling the person directly and sometimes ghosting (often it was sufficient to hit the "unfollow" button). It has never been personal, and it doesn't mean they are inherently bad humans, nor does it mean I hold them in a bad place in my heart. Some reminded me of or encouraged bad behaviors. Some reminded me too much of bad situations from my past. Some simply talked too much trash. They were life-taking to me.

The great news is that ridding yourself of the life-taking allows for investment in existing and new life-giving fountains. By focusing on the most positive of my friendships, I've found depth in those relationships and immersion into their networks. By pursuing basketball, the guitar, and God, I've joined and explored new communities and tapped into new levels of achievement. I've stopped pretending to like baseball and poured myself into hockey. That's a heck of a sport. Perhaps living in the city of the two-time Stanley Cup champions helped.

I miss people. I miss places. I miss some of the old times. I grieve for them. I write out lists of what I miss, and I question the sentiments. I ask myself if I really loved them or just loved the idea of them. It helps.

CHAPTER 23

SWEET CHILD O' MINE

I've always wanted kids. I have especially wanted a little boy. I'd love a girl, too, but the boy is who I always think about. I've concocted intricate plans to dress and equip him with accessories that make him the coolest kid in the neighborhood. I've devised a game that starts the day he can stand, in which I provide a prize for each time he knocks over a soda can by throwing a ball between his legs. Hence, he becomes an outstanding long snapper and gets a college scholarship and NFL riches. I also want a permanent best friend who has no choice but to hang out with me for several years. And, very importantly, I want to be the absolute best dad of all time.

I've never been married; therefore, in a traditional sense, I have not been very close to having a kid. And if I'm honest with myself, until my recent life change, I'd been terrified of having kids. Being responsible for a human life would have been a rather impenetrable cap on my ability to get up and go anywhere and do anything I want. It would have been tough to get the green light to follow Bruce through Europe for a few weeks with a baby. It also would have been a severe hindrance to my ability to self-medicate.

In the spring of 2022, as I was hurtling into a stay at a mental facility, I received life-altering and pants-soiling news. My friend Lindsay, with whom I'd had a fun night months earlier, informed me that she was pregnant. Being that there had been medically reliable contraception methods in place, my instinct was to congratulate her and mentally (not out loud) speculate on who the father was. She calmly informed me that I was the only option, and since she is an infallibly honest woman, I trusted that we would be sharing a living souvenir from that intimate moment in our history.

In the worst of my meltdown, I absorbed a series of emotional haymakers. Sheer terror bled into absolute panic, which jammed into a healthy dose of disbelief and denial. Over time, a tidal wave of shame and all-consuming guilt took hold for several weeks. I never imagined I'd be the guy who had a child with someone who wasn't my wife. I was also facing the prospect of several extremely uncomfortable conversations with friends, family, and a very specific person I would hurt severely. I was thankful to be inside a safe place where I couldn't hurt myself to escape the agony.

And you'd better believe I hit Google and WebMD very hard. I unearthed a comprehensive set of medical conditions that could trigger a false positive on a pregnancy test. The odds were miniscule that multiple tests would show pregnancy when there was no baby. For days, I held out for the possibility that it was all a mistake. Desperate emotions were overpowering my logical, analytical brain and the obvious outcome.

Blood tests confirmed the pregnancy. In one of the best decisions of all time, Lindsay and I made a firm commitment to see this life to its fulfillment. We determined that while we would not be romantically attached, this new life was bigger than our personal needs and would have two loving parents.

For the first week inside the ward, I withheld this information from everyone. My secrecy only magnified the shame and confusion I felt. In a group therapy session on a Thursday, I shared the full spectrum of my psychological context, including my future as a father. The warmth and caring that I felt from my cohort was genuine and consistent. I kept hearing that from what they knew of me, I would be an amazing father, particularly from Pablo who was another "young at heart" daddy. I remember in one of our afternoon group check-ins, the icebreaker question was to describe the best day of each patient's life. For everyone except me, it was the day that their first child was born. It may not have been the required thirty data points for statistical significance, but I believed the sample to be conclusive: I had a wonderful moment and lifetime of experiences ahead.

In the following weeks, the fear and exasperation evolved into anticipation and excitement, with a healthy dose of "how in the world are we going to do this?" My baby became the voice in my head to work harder at the clinic (to leave it all on the field, so to speak) to prepare myself for fatherhood. It wasn't just me in the transformation boat anymore. Now I had a very high-priority VIP passenger.

On my way out the door, I was infinitely more prepared to be a daddy (for Excel nerds, it was technically a "DIV#0!" error because my starting point was zero). It was the biggest difference in the life I was walking back into versus the one I left behind. I am so thankful for the timing of the pregnancy news vis-à-vis the meltdown and the admission to the facility. This little baby gave me permanent reinforcement to continue down the path of healthy living and fulfilling God's will.

In the first weeks home, I nervously informed the rest of my family about what was to come. While I was full of shame and fear of judgment, their reaction couldn't have been more positive. Confused, yes, but positive. Above all, they were excited for something to rally our weirdly structured family tree, someone to love and upon whom to dote. Of course, there were also some very gut-wrenching conversations with people who were shocked and hurt by the news. Sadly, I wasn't able to have all these conversations directly, as the gossip mill of South Tampa is fast and furious.

In the weeks between mid-June and mid-July (months four and five of the pregnancy), the baby preparation accelerated. Lindsay and I developed a responsible and healthy way of working together. She and I put any friction we may have aside to only focus on providing the best life for this child. One night, some friends of hers did a gender reveal for just the two of us. My heart burst when blue confetti erupted onto my kitchen island and confirmed what I had so hoped was true.

God unlocked badges in my heart as a daddy. Quite a few settings in my soul have been adjusted permanently. I felt a type of love I've never experienced. I finally understood what my mom had been talking about for years, why she still holds her arm over my chest when she hits the brakes or asks me to text her when I land after my two hundredth flight of the calendar year. I would do anything to protect that baby. I have pictured an entire life with him. I went home early one night last week because whatever I was doing couldn't compare to the idea of snuggling with my boy, even though my boy wasn't born yet.

There's also a dad setting that must be sponsored by Northwestern Mutual, Home Depot, and Amazon. I thought much more about efficient financial instruments and finance education. I made adjustments and planned for intense babyproofing of my egregiously unsafe home and pool. I admired baby strollers and travel accessories that looked comfortable, effective, and somewhat cool. Personally, the most shocking behavior I exhibited was newfound admiration for midsize crossover SUVs.

Any molecule of the fear, terror, and shame that I felt disappeared and gave way to joy, gratitude, and downright pumped-upness. My little boy would be something to hold and love as a beautiful byproduct of a really bad stretch of my life. He would be the super glue that permanently cemented my mental health transformation work. I was so thankful to have this gift.

They say there's a parental instinct for when something is wrong with your child. I experienced that for the first time yesterday. I woke up anxious after a night of terrible dreams involving kids. Around nine last night, I was on a flight and got a "when are you home" text from Lindsay. We didn't communicate like that. I knew in my heart that something was wrong. At 10:30 p.m. last night, I learned that my boy's little heart gave out five months into the pregnancy.

Lindsay and I spent the entire night crying, questioning, and sharing. We told stories about the last several months. We reminisced, if that's what you'd call it, about our panic in those first weeks. We rotated between silence, inconsolable tears, and laughs. There is no pain that I have felt that can stand toe to toe with what I feel right now.

And you'd better believe I'm hitting Google and WebMD very hard. I have sought to unearth a comprehensive set of medical conditions that would obscure the sound of a healthy, beating heart. There aren't any. But I'm still irrationally holding out for the possibility that this is all a mistake. Desperate emotions are overpowering my logical, analytical brain and the obvious outcome.

I'm trying to find the positive in this experience. It's not easy to locate. All I can think is that I'm being given an opportunity to put what I learned at the psych ward into action. I'm living in the moment today and not projecting the weeks, months, and years ahead with an emotional hole in them. I'm practicing mindfulness to remind myself to live in the now and not borrow the pain that will come. I'm following my daily schedule extra closely to keep out the bad habits that threaten me around each corner. I'm gravitating toward life-giving with a trip to Atlanta to be with Elizabeth and her family.

I am proud of myself for handling it in the way that I have. I'm avoiding the trash on which I would have leaned in my former life. I'm getting stronger—dare I say, I'm feeling some swagger. The world can't hit me much harder than it has, and I'm still standing (you're thinking about Elton John, aren't you?). It's okay to be unimaginably sad and feel invincibly strong at the same time. I've never experienced this before today.

Archie Campbell Stutts loved strawberries. His mother craved them constantly while he was growing, so it could only mean he was eager for them. He was a little fella at the start, measuring a bit small early on. But he was feisty—early on, he vanquished a loitering twin sharing the womb with him (à la Dwight Schrute). He loved his mommy so much. He gave her the joy of anticipating a baby who would undoubtedly be perfect. He loved his daddy so much. He inspired him to be a better man and grow closer to God. He wanted him to be a hero to his son for a long time and never again come close to throwing his life away.

Once dad mode is activated, it doesn't go back. I miss him to a degree and depth that I can never explain in words. My only comforts are sleeping with his Carolina Panthers onesie that I bought him weeks ago and knowing he's with his namesake great-grandfather and my dad. I can't wait to meet Archie one day and show him the man he made me become.

CHAPTER 24

TOUGHER THAN THE REST

I have a lot of recurring dreams. There are scary ones about tornadoes and plane crashes. There are vaguely aspirational ones, like the time I was dating Kelly Clarkson. Most frequently, though, I dream I'm in a place or with a person with whom I have unfinished business.

For the most part, I've had the option to resolve these dreams in real life, simply through in-person visits or conversations. But that would be too easy. Instead, I turned the stars of my subconscious into mythical figures and monuments that I obsessed over. I had no desire for closure. Instead, I let the fantasy of a chance encounter with these people and places (along with the possible outcomes) overrule real-world resolution.

But now, I'm tired of old houses and acquaintances dominating my subconscious. I want new dreams. And so, while I was inside the clinic, I reached out to a former girlfriend and best friend (same person) with whom I'd had no contact whatsoever for ten years. We hadn't exchanged as much as a text since the day I found out she was engaged via a Google search. For a full decade, I imagined what I would say or do if I saw her. I dreamed of hangouts, of irrational reconciliations, of chance encounters that I would win or lose. I replayed over and over the time that I actually did see her pushing a stroller in a small Michigan town where I was visiting. I couldn't have scripted that one. I panicked and hid.

I sent a note to an ancient email address of hers. She responded the same day. A few days later, we were on the phone. I told her where I was. She told me about her wonderful family, and we laughed as if not a day had passed. We didn't need to litigate what had happened a lifetime ago. We needed only a reconnection as friendly adults who have dumb and perfect senses of humor. We text a few times a week now. I look forward to meeting her husband and kids one day. She got out of my dreams and into my phone (you're thinking of Billy Ocean, aren't you?).

Since then, I've been on a mission to slay my false idols and holograms. I've done a good job reaching out to some people and having chats that were long overdue. I've visited a few old haunts and discovered that they're made of wood, brick, and below-code fixtures. I've even visited a certain creek that's not quite as navigable as it once was (due to erosion of dirt).

My largest mental monument is the first home in which I lived, the two-story, rectangular, brick masterpiece that is 811 Museum Drive. This was the only house where our nuclear family was intact, the house where the divorce conversations happened, the yard where all of our stuff was strewn on moving day when I was six years old. Over the last thirty-five years, I've probably had two hundred dreams in which I unexpectedly find myself there. Sometimes I'm lost while walking and end up there. Occasionally, someone I know lives there. I've even moved back in once or twice. In every case, I'm mesmerized by the inside. I look for marks that prove my former residency, and I feel a connection to a life that was gone a long time ago.

For decades, I have irrationally imagined a fantasy life in which there was no divorce, no split lives—just a tight nuclear support structure. That alternate reality has stability, predictability, and safety. I wonder if, with these guardrails intact, I would have avoided my two meltdowns, whether the first half of my life would have been a steady line and not the wild-amplitude adventure I've had. I sometimes feel mad, resentful, or sorry for myself. I have often chased this idea, spinning myself into a completely unproductive loop.

The very symbol of that parallel universe has been this house.

Three weeks after I left my temporary home in the psych ward, I decided to put an end to the obsession. On June 11, I made a cold-call knock on the door that I used to race in and out of as a toddler. Though there were signs of life, to no surprise of mine, there was no response. I wouldn't have answered either, and not just because my rental car was an orange Altima. I left a note explaining who I was and that I'd love to take a look inside. I left my phone number, and the woman living there texted a few hours later offering an open door and a welcome tour.

Hours later, I was greeted with smiles, warmth, and a genuine sense of curiosity about me and the history of the house. As soon as I crossed the threshold, it became clear that this was just a house, not a temple to historicizing the demise of the Stutts family.

I walked room to room with the mom and the teenage daughter of the resident family. I told stories. I found the spot in the living room where the Christmas tree stood. I pointed out the bathroom in which I'd locked myself and gone into a full meltdown, not realizing I had the power to unlock it. We went to my bedroom, where I demonstrated how I laid on my left side while in bed so I could see my parents' television to watch *Cheers* and *Moonlighting* with no sound. I crawled into the space under the dormer window, where every day I had kept watch for Elizabeth coming home from school. The kitchen where my mom cooked flowed into the garage where the Buick wagon and Fiat Spider were once parked.

The house had a lot of good and bad memories. They're only images and moments of a life that has been long left behind.

Now the house was filled with new spirit and life. It was changed to become better, more modern, and more livable. I couldn't find the candle wax once deposited on the windowsills at Christmas. The '70s-toned walls were painted or removed to bring light and openness. The backyard, once big enough for touch football games, had been shrunk to accommodate an absolutely perfect brick outdoor living space. The dad, his teenage sons, and some friends were watching baseball; they offered me a seat and a beer. I declined. I felt like an outsider, like an old friend who was imposing. I didn't feel sad but happy that the house had moved on.

I finally confirmed that there's nothing magical or fantastical about this house. There's no portal to an alternate reality, nor is there any need for one. My experiences have all led to where I am now—a dude who has a lot of time ahead of him and the wisdom to live those years well.

It was time for me to move on from a fantasy. I felt free to do so.

This house was born in the 1970s. Its DNA is rooted in the hands of my grandfather and his crew. The fingerprints of my family, our good times and our mistakes, may yet rest in a few far-flung corners. But it has a new life and isn't stuck in the past.

I used to think of this house as old. Now I think of it as experienced, ever evolving, and distinguished.

That house has a lot of years ahead of it. It'll be cool to see how it changes.

ACKNOWLEDGMENTS

I t's kind of hard to thank people for supporting me along the book writing process because I didn't intend to write a book. This document was meant for me to memorialize my thoughts, accelerate my healing, and pass the time as an unemployed guy. For six weeks I typed away at Armature Works in Tampa, Florida, dressed in my finest athleisure, mingling among the moms, kids, and work-from-homers in a loud, trendy food hall. Writing gave me purpose when purpose eluded me.

I wrote this thing in a psychological fever dream with a furious explosion of hunt-and-peck typing and streams of consciousness. And then it got massaged into a book. And now here we are.

I'm thankful to God for blessing me with the bumps of the past several months and years to change and prepare me for a killer second half of my life. I also recognize that He blessed me with the resources to invest in the medical care I needed. I ask that He multiplies the resources of those in need to afford them the opportunity I had to get better.

Publishing this bad boy turned out to be quite an adventure that is worthy of another book. Skipping to the end, a talented group of individuals across two publishers patiently guided me through this process. Ryan Garcia, Jason Arias, and Cristina "Wednesday" Ricci set the foundation. Then, Kat Dixon, Andy Symonds, and the whole team at Ballast Books brought it home. This crew gave me the perfect balance of positive encouragement and realistic perspective. Namely, they reminded me that nobody would understand the ridiculous pop culture references that they wisely deleted.

My mom, Barbara, has been gracious in letting me tell the story of our family in an uncensored voice. I genuinely hope it echoes the unconditional, immeasurable, and sometimes undeserved amount of love that she has for my sister and me. Without that love I wouldn't feel safe putting myself all the way out there like this. I know that if everyone else runs away, she'll still be there.

I hope this book honors my late father, Clyde, a man who gave me so many gifts and I know is proud of me today. Retired bankers all over Charlotte tell me how much a look like and remind them of my dad. I take it as a compliment. I've learned more about him in the time he's been gone than when I knew him alive. I appreciate him more by the day.

And, of course, thanks to my stepmother, Michele, and my stepfather, Mike, plus, of course, my li'l sibs, Jonathan and Courtney, for absorbing the cringes related to digging up the past. We are a fantastic modern family.

Big thanks to my friend, sporting event sherpa, and brother, Tom. He changed the trajectory of my career for good and supported me when

I fell down. They say you don't make great friends after college. They're wrong. And there are so many other friends I could name. You know who you are, and I appreciate your nonjudgmental support. Except for when I get bad haircuts (or, in my case, no haircut at all for a year, in which case the judgment came swiftly).

If this book is bad, you can blame Ms. Wilder, one of the most influential teachers in my life. She is responsible for giving me the confidence and courage to creatively write and share the results. In high school, she read my silly stories, heartfelt attempts at emotional text, and earnest musings about literature and pushed me further. She was the first person to tell me I was a good writer and that I should explore my voice.

Big thanks to an important group that I won't mention by name with whom I spent several weeks at a place I won't say where. Without them, the story of living in medical captivity would be a lot bleaker and sadder. I miss all of you. I think of you often, and I wish continued recovery to each of you. I remember special things about each one of you and hope one day our paths cross (but not at the same place). And a special message just for you: "Take your masks; leave your phones."

Finally, Elizabeth, without whom I'm not sure where I'd be right now. She brought a rational process to my irrational chaos. I hope this book shows her how much she's impacted my life. May we have many more years of laughing, watching plane crash shows, and going to music festivals like cool adults.

And thank you to anyone who read this book. Please pass your copy along to someone else who might need it.